INTERM

lei
& tourism

INTERMEDIATE
leisure & tourism

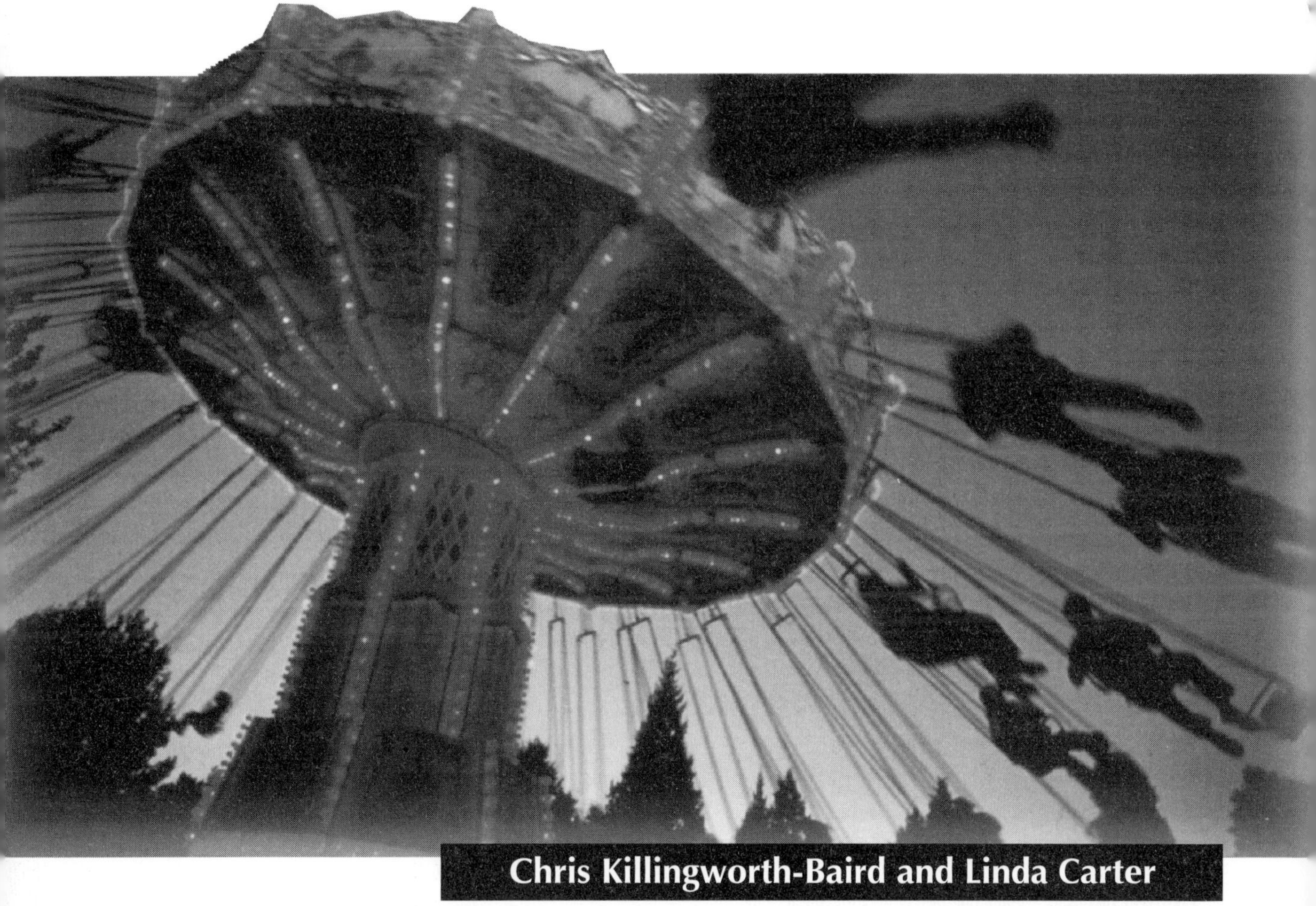

Chris Killingworth-Baird and Linda Carter

Hodder & Stoughton
A MEMBER OF THE HODDER HEADLINE GROUP

British Library Cataloguing in Publication Data
Baird, Chris
Intermediate leisure & tourism
1. Tourist trade – Great Britain 2. Leisure industry – Great Britain
3. Tourist trade – Great Britain – Problems, exercises, etc. 4. Leisure industry – Great Britain – Problems, exercises, etc.
I. Title II. Carter, Linda
338.4'791

ISBN 0 340 64413 3

First published 1996
Impression number 10 9 8 7 6 5 4 3 2 1
Year 1999 1998 1997 1996

Typeset by Wearset, Boldon, Tyne and Wear.
Printed in Great Britain for Hodder & Stoughton Educational, a division of Hodder Headline Plc, 338 Euston Road, London NW1 3BH
by the Bath Press, Bath

contents

Introduction *vii*

Acknowledgements *ix*

1 Investigating the leisure and tourism industries 1
- Investigating the leisure and recreation industry 1
- Investigating the travel and tourism industries 5
- Preparing for employment in the leisure and tourism industries 12

2 Marketing and promoting leisure and tourism products 33
- Investigating marketing and promotion in leisure and recreation and travel and tourism organisations 33
- Planning a leisure and recreation or travel and tourism promotional campaign 43
- Running and evaluating a leisure or tourism promotional campaign 46

3 Customer service in leisure and tourism 50
- Explaining the principles of customer service in leisure and tourism 50
- Investigating the provision of information as part of customer service 55
- Investigating and demonstrating sales techniques as part of customer service 58
- Providing and evaluating customer service in leisure and tourism 59

4 Contributing to the running of an event 72
- Planning an event with others 72
- Undertaking a role in the team event 73
- Evaluating the team event 75

Index 79

introduction

Each of the first three units of this book concludes with a set of questions and a case study which can be used to test yourself. The following tips will help you with these.

Exam technique

Like everything else, it is possible to learn how to pass exams. Obviously there is no substitute for knowledge, but there are lots of ways to improve how you present your knowledge, and various techniques to enable you to make the best of your time.

1 MULTIPLE CHOICE

Remember, here you have a 1 in 4 chance of being right, so *always* have a go. Good multiple choice questions will always include an alternative choice that is *similar* to the correct one, or at least another possible solution, so *take your time*: there are no prizes for being first. Select the answer you think is correct, then try all the others, examine them and try to decide why the one you have selected is correct.

Words in exams are really important (more about this later). Look at the following example.

The best way to ensure that customers return to a facility is to:

a keep the prices low
b send them regular information
c provide value for money
d keep introducing new features

Now the key word here is *best*, and it means that although the other ways *may* contribute to a customer returning, only one way is *best*, so you must eliminate as follows:

a Low prices are good, we all know, but low prices might indicate poor quality.
b Regular information is useful, keeps you up to date with what is happening and keeps reminding customers that you exist.
c Value for money is good – we all like to think that we are spending our money wisely.
d New features are interesting, but they will not all interest everyone, and ultimately they must cost more.

Thus, the *best* answer in this case is 'c'.

Try to use this method of selection when you are not sure – it often helps. Above all, take your time, read all the choices through, then make a choice, check the others again and, once you have finished your paper, read them all through again and check once more.

2 EXAM WORDS

Short-answer questions all contain a verb which tells you what to do: 'Describe', 'State', 'List', etc. This tells you, or should tell you, how detailed the answer needs to be. If the questions say 'List', you need only give a few words in a numbered list, thus:

1
2
3
4

If you write all you know about the subject here, you will get no extra marks – in fact, the examiner will probably be so frustrated trying to find the answer that they may not give you your possible mark.

Take the following example:

Over the weekend you went out with some friends to a new club. You met someone new, spent the evening with them and got home very late. You will be meeting again on Wednesday evening.

1. You may *describe* the events of the evening to your best friend, with plenty of detail and few omissions.
2. If you were asked in class what you did, you may *summarise* the evening.
3. You would probably give your parents an *outline* of the main points.
4. If you *state* what you did, it is probably to your parents – i.e. you give a very brief account where you went and what you did.
5. You could *list* the people you saw at the club.
6. You might *compare* the club with the one you usually go to.
7. You could *give* a friend several reasons for trying it out.
8. If you *evaluate* your experience, you will be deciding if it was worth the money.
9. You might *explain* to a friend what you most enjoyed about the evening.

Remember, always look for those key words: the verbs, or doing words. They tell you how much or little is expected in the answer.

Finally, if there are marks published, use those also as a guide: if the question carries two marks, you needn't write two pages, especially if the next question carries 10 marks. *Usually* (but not always), two marks means you have to make *two points*. For example:

Question: give ways in which a facility can promote customer satisfaction.

(2 marks)

Your answer:

1. Ensuring staff are polite and helpful.
2. Providing value for money.

See – it's easy when you know how!

acknowledgements

The authors and publisher would like to thank the following for permission to use material in this publication:

The Automobile Association (AA); Roger Vlitos; Edwardian Radisson Hotels; the British Airports Authority (BAA); Jarvis Hotels; the British Tourist Authority (BTA); Madame Tussaud's; Cunard Line; the HCIMA Yearbook; Lucozade; the Market Research Society (MRS); Forte (UK) Limited; Colchester Zoo; the Royal Botanic Gardens Kew; Allsport (UK) Ltd; Granada Studios Tour; Britannia; Thomson; P&O European Ferries; and the Aeneas Hotel in Cyprus.

unit 1

Investigating the leisure and tourism industries

At the end of this unit, you should have:

I investigated local and national aspects of the leisure and recreation industry

II investigated local and national aspects of the travel and tourism industry

III investigated and prepared for available employment opportunities in these industries.

The leisure and tourism industries are growth industries, which is good for our economy and good for your future employment. One of the things that makes them growth industries is the way in which they mean different things to different people. This also makes them hard to define accurately – we can find very many definitions, some we may agree with, some that are not so appealing.

Investigating the leisure and recreation industry

Let us first examine the idea of leisure and recreation. Leisure and recreation could mean lots of different things, and my idea of each of the following may well be different from yours. Leisure might be:

- a sports activity of some sort
- some spare time enjoyed after college or work
- a social event
- a hobby

The main point about this list, which is by no means complete, is that it implies a *choice*.

Figure 1.1 A young family enjoying their leisure time together.

activity

1. List five leisure activities in which you regularly take part. Calculate approximately how much each costs you in a month, and say which ones are limited by the cost factor.
2. Give an example of a leisure activity with no cost.
3. List some form of recreation which is a group activity.
4. Give one example of a leisure pastime where you do not need to be with friends.
5. What would you like to do if money were no object?

One of the most important things, then, about leisure time is that it is personal to each individual, and that they can dispose of it how they wish.

Would it be accurate to say that our leisure time is equivalent to our *disposable* time? Not entirely, because some classes of people have far more disposable time than others (the unemployed for example) but would not, in most cases, consider themselves *at leisure* for all of this time. It is also difficult to define leisure exclusively as the free time after work. In some cases, work is clearly defined. You may have a Saturday job where you work from 9 am to 6 pm. When you finish work, your time is your own. You might eat something, shower, change and then go out with your friends, and at *this* point, you might feel your leisure time is just beginning.

For some people, the eating of a meal is itself a leisure activity. For someone who has travelled all day, or a long way, a long hot soak in a bath is not functional, it is leisurely.

What about a mother? When do her working hours finish? Such hours are not clearly defined – a mother is always 'on call'. If there are small children, they will want to play. Is this recreation for the mother? It is difficult to decide whether, from the mother's point of view, playing with a child is a duty or is something which is a choice.

Play is an important part of leisure. At an early age, you

Figure 1.2 Children learning through play at school.

go to a 'play group', and then you learn how to play a musical instrument or a game of squash. And later, you may choose to go to the theatre instead of the cinema. Like leisure time, playtime has no firm definition, and its chief characteristic is that it involves free choice: no one can force you to play. Play may enable you to 'let off steam', wear yourself out, make new friends, learn new things. In short, not only is it fun but it is often educational as well. Children at play learn to develop their talents and to mix with others of a similar age group. Playtime at school serves not only as a break from lessons but also as a very important part of the growing-up (or socialisation) process.

activity

Working with the person next to you, briefly discuss, and prepare to report back on, what you think leisure time would mean to the following people:

1. a 10-year-old boy
2. your tutor
3. a jockey
4. a bank manager.

THE PUBLIC, PRIVATE AND VOLUNTARY SECTORS

Quite clearly, all the people mentioned in the activity above will have different ways of spending their free time.

This is because we live in a society which has a mixed economy, and consequently different categories of providers exist in order to cater for all our needs.

The public sector originally existed in order to provide a service for the community – most communities had, for example, a swimming pool. Increasingly now, although it is still an important provider for the community, the public sector has also to be profit-motivated in much of its work.

The *private* sector has always had profit high on its agenda. Organisations in this sector are usually owned by large companies, private individuals or groups of individuals who have joined together for business purposes. Providers in this sector see a need for a facility, take a risk on their investment, and hope to make a profit while providing a service.

Many profit-making organisations may choose at some time to organise an event that either takes place on behalf of a charity or is *sponsored* by a charity, with a view to making a profit. Charities are dependent not only on such fund-raising activities but also on government grants, and the recent allocation to the Arts Council of funds from the National Lottery is increasingly seen as a source of revenue.

Grants are a great asset for any industry, and they are often available for leisure and tourism from a variety of organisations, ranging from central government departments to private companies wishing to promote their name through sponsorship. Examples of government bodies that award grants to the leisure and tourism industries include:

- the British Tourist Board
- the Arts Council of Great Britain
- the Countryside Commission
- the Sports Council

activity

Can you add some more organisations to this list?

Grants are also available, on some occasions, from European sources for the development of tourism in a particular area, or for the development of leisure and recreation in a *deprived* area. Sometimes these grants are only available if the money is spent in a certain way, and sometimes they are 'match funded', which means the European fund pays one half and the local authority or equivalent pays the other half.

There are a number of reasons why *voluntary organisations* emerge, and these are frequently related to demand or to some other analysis of needs. The organisation may provide a particular service, for example the creation of a society of like-minded people. The main factor which holds such groups together is that they are not primarily profit-motivated, and that any profit is viewed as surplus funds to be returned and used for further activity. Many voluntary organisations are efficient fund-raisers and generate income in a variety of ways, including:

- events (e.g. quiz nights)
- subscriptions
- fees (e.g. entrance fees)
- sponsorship
- grants

Some large organisations (e.g. the Royal Society for the Prevention of Cruelty to Animals (RSPCA)) have official charitable status, and consequently encourage people to leave them donations in their will, which enable them to claim additional benefit through tax relief.

Within each major town in the UK, there are examples of leisure facilities which come from the public, private or voluntary sectors. Remember that the public sector is largely funded by central or local government; that the private sector involves commercial operations that aim to make a profit; and that the voluntary sector involves organisations and facilities that are managed and operated largely by volunteers and that are frequently non-profit-making or hold charitable status.

activity

Make a list of leisure and tourism facilities in your local area, highlighting which belong to:

1. the public sector
2. the private sector
3. the voluntary sector.

Make enquiries about whether any of the facilities in the previous list received grants in the last 12 months. If so, were there any conditions, and where were the grants received from?

CHOOSING AN ACTIVITY

The individual's choice of a leisure activity is usually influenced by family or friends (the peer group) or both. Many activities are undertaken as part of a group, e.g. cinema visits, swimming, contact sport, Scouts and Guides. Availability and location are also usually amongst the reasons for choice, as is the frequency of a particular activity.

activity

Compare two facilities, in your locality, which offer the same or a similar activity. Look at both activities in detail and state which is the most favourable, giving your reasons.

The main points which you should have considered in the above activity might include:

- location
- transport
- availability
- frequency
- timing
- price
- membership
- fees
- specialist clothing
- equipment (hire)

All of the things on this list are points which may contribute to the success of any amenity. In addition, of course, the potential client must have an *interest* in the service on offer, and they also need to feel confident that they could *learn* there: many clients may be reluctant to join the club if they are beginners and everyone else is advanced. It is also important for facility managers to check if there is another potential market in addition to the one which is already being satisfied.

SECURITY MATTERS

It does not matter how attractive an establishment is if it is not a safe or secure place to be in, because customers need to feel safe in order to relax and enjoy themselves. Security facilities could involve something as simple as adequate lighting in the car part or a secure place to deposit personal belongings. Regarding the latter, many leisure facilities offer a wide variety of ways in which customers can secure their belongings, ranging from baskets, which may be under the supervision of an attendant, to individual safes or lockers for which there may well be a small charge (which is often refundable). Hotels, on their part, are required by law to provide safe deposit facilities for guests' valuables. These could range from a system whereby the main hotel safe is used, to a secure room giving the guest access by key to their box in privacy. In addition, there will be a notice in the bedroom, and usually at reception, stating that if a guest's property is not placed in the safe, the establishment cannot be held responsible for loss or damage to that item. Of course, in all establishments there will also, in certain areas, be disclaimer notices which remove liability for loss or damage from the establishment. A car park is one such area, a coat rail in a restaurant is another. Finally, once a customer is reassured that their personal belongings are safe, they need to feel that *they themselves* are safe: all customers should be aware of fire exits and fire notices, and of what action to take in the event of a fire practice or the discovery of a fire.

Any establishment which is selling products and services to customers must ensure that it is a safe and clean place for its staff and visitors. Depending on the type of establishment, some employees will have basic first-aid training, and some places such as a large hotel may have a nurse on the premises for the well-being of staff and guests. Any swimming pool must have in attendance a qualified lifeguard who will also have first-aid training.

By law, companies with a certain number of employees have to have an accident book in which any accident to either an employee or a customer must be recorded. This information may be used at a later date for further treatment, compensation or insurance claims. An establishment is also required to keep a well-stocked first-aid box, in a location known to its employees, in case of a minor accident.

a c t i v i t y

List suggested contents for a first-aid box. Is there one somewhere at your place of study? How does your list compare with the contents of that box?

Can you think of any additional items you would perhaps include for use by:

1 an overseas tour rep
2 a football coach
3 senior citizens holiday operator.

(Why do people who work in kitchens have to wear blue plasters if they cut themselves?)

Investigating the travel and tourism industries

Earlier in this unit, we asked what leisure time might mean to a bank manager. Would their answer be the same as that of a hotel manager? Probably not. The reason, of course, has to do with the type of hours that hotel staff work.

Tourism never stops: the travel and tourism industry goes on 24 hours a day for seven days of the week. Even on Christmas Day, when most leisure outlets are closed, some sectors in tourism are operational, and very busy.

To define tourism is almost as hard as it is to define leisure. In this case the problem is: where does it start, and where does it stop. Tourism is usually defined as the movement of people from one place to another, people engaged in activities which involve spending time away from home. The main point to remember is that the visit or stay is of a temporary nature. In its broadest definition, tourism includes the booking before the travel, the actual travel, the stay away from home, activities carried out whilst away from home, and the return trip.

a c t i v i t y

Before reading on, list some organisations which you think would be involved in the tourism sector as defined above.

You probably thought of:

- travel agents
- hotels
- bus/train operators
- plane operators

You may also have included:

- hotel booking agents
- tourist information centre
- taxi operators
- ferry operators
- holiday camps
- tourist attractions
- sports centres
- swimming pools

and there are many more.

The idea of tourism often conjures up an image of *holiday-makers*, either in this country or abroad. This is because of the link between the tourism industry and package tours. As you have seen, however, the concept of tourism is much broader than this, and can apply just as easily to someone who travels for business purposes as it does to someone who travels for holiday or leisure purposes.

Tourism traffic is not all one-way either. While we are busy leaving the UK for various reasons, people are also arriving. This is known as *incoming tourism*. Movement within the country (e.g. someone from Birmingham visiting the Lake District) is known as *domestic tourism*.

Some forms of tourism are closely linked to leisure, and of course the reverse is also true. There are often special holidays or weekend breaks arranged for people who

Figure 1.3 Gatwick Airport – open for business 365 days a year.

share common interests, e.g. the arts and entertainment, or heritage weekends where the trip is linked to a particular activity or tourist attraction. This is an excellent way of building business out of people's leisure interests, and it is good for both the consumer and the business since, regardless of whether the offer involves a leisure product or a tourism service, the appeal of *both* areas can now be combined.

Leisure and tourism facilities are far superior in certain cities and towns than in others. This may be due to the population size or the amount of money available. Perhaps an event is run on a national or international basis, and with advertising and sponsorship a major source of income, certain cities and towns will have a larger budget, or greater marketing muscle, than others.

Wine Tasting Weekends

A WEEKEND TO TRY AND REMEMBER...!

Whether you enjoy the odd slurp or are a mature imbiber, here's an opportunity to spend a weekend of wine tasting and discovery at the Jarvis Great Danes Hotel, Maidstone (p 31). You'll be able to taste the best that the Vine can offer from both the New and Old world in a relaxed, friendly atmosphere.

The Programme

- **Begin on Friday** by celebrating the end of the week with a tasting of Champagnes and sparkling wines.
- **Saturday morning** involves either a trip to Denbies, England's largest wine estate (April & September), or Leeds Castle (November). Both trips include a tour, lunch and tasting.

There's no let up! More tastings on

- **Saturday evening** As with Friday night you will be guided through the wines by Michael Hooley, who has a wealth of knowledge as both a wine professional and consumer.
- **Sunday morning** Just when you thought it was safe.... another tasting awaits you followed by a quiz - to see how much you remember.

Dates and Prices

12-14 April 96
13-15 September 96
22-24 November 96

£139 per person
The price includes:

- Three course dinner, bed and breakfast on Friday & Saturday
- All wine tasting
- Saturday trip to Denbies Wine Estate or Leeds Castle
- Sunday Lunch
- Free use of Sebastian Coe Health Park

Fine Antique Weekends

Whether you are a serious collector or the owner of a few treasured pieces, here's an opportunity to learn, enjoy and appreciate more about antiques with the help of our very own antiques expert at the Jarvis Rivenhall Hotel, Colchester (p65).

The Programme

Friday After dinner, gather to hear an introduction to your weekend from our Antiques Expert.

Saturday After breakfast your morning is free to enjoy visiting the Antique Shops in the nearby villages of Kelvedon and Coggeshall. At 2.00pm in the hotel, you are invited to bring your own antique to our very own "Antiques Roadshow" for valuation and information.

Sunday After breakfast your chance to show your own expertise as you put a price on some fifteen items (you'll be given a few tips from our Expert) with prizes for the winners.

Dates & Prices

1 - 3 Nov 96

£99 per person including 2 nights dinner, bed and breakfast

Steam Railway Breaks

Journey back in time on a Pacific Class Steam Locomotive and explore the Crewe Heritage Centre.

This short break will be based at the Jarvis Crewe Arms (p67), originally a Victorian railway hostelry.

The Programme

- Three course dinner, accomodation for one night and full English breakfast.
- Return ticket between Crewe and either Holyhead, Glasgow or Carlisle by Steam and Electric locomotive
- Service & VAT at 17.5%
- Children under 16 years can stay free in parents room. You need only pay for meals and £35 for a childs price rail ticket.

Dates & Prices

25 May 1996
8 June 1996
6 July 1996
20 July 1996
27 July 1996

£95.75 per person

Racing Breaks at Newmarket

Enjoy a weekend at the races whilst staying at the Smoke House Inn, Mildenhall (p63).

The Programme

- 2 nights Dinner, Bed and Breakfast
- A guided tour of Newmarket
  - Trainers Yard
  - The Gallops
  - Horseracing Museum
- Entrance to the members enclosure and racecard on a race day.
- Transport to and from the track.

Dates & Prices

3 - 5 May 96
31 May - 2 Jun 96
21 - 23 Jun 96
28 Jun - 1 Jul 96
19 - 21 Jul 96
26 - 28 Jul 96
2 - 4 Aug 96
23 - 25 Aug 96
27 - 29 Sep 96
11 - 13 Oct 96
25 - 27 Oct 96

£189 per person

Figure 1.4 Examples of leisure breaks from Embassy/Jarvis Hotels.

activity

1 Refer to the following list of towns/cities:

- London
- Manchester
- Glasgow
- Edinburgh
- Cardiff
- Birmingham
- Blackpool
- Bournemouth
- Cambridge
- Oxford
- Leeds
- Nottingham

Name either an event which takes place on an annual basis or a well-known exhibition centre for each.

2 Some international events take place in the UK annually and some occasionally. Give two examples of each, and state where they are held.

3 Manchester put in a bid to hold the Olympic games. As a result, their facilities were upgraded and should now be amongst some of the best in the world. State why you think Manchester would have been a good choice. What major problems, if any, do you think there might have been with Manchester as an Olympic destination? Could you suggest any other location within the UK that would be able to host the Olympic Games? If so, give your reasons.

Within every major town and some smaller towns there are one or more *travel agents*. This is due to the increase in people taking holidays. These may be day trips, weekend breaks or UK or overseas travel. Within your local area, you may find a travel agent which belongs to a national company which has branches in most towns/cities, and you may also find a travel agent which is independently owned and run, with perhaps only one shop.

activity

Give two examples of each type of travel agent in your local area, and list the main activities of both. Compare the range of services offered. Which travel agent do you feel gives the best service, choice/range and price? What other reasons would affect your choice when wishing to book a holiday? You may wish to conduct a survey showing the difference between services available from different travel agents within your area. Using the following headings:

- package holidays
- currency exchange
- rail bookings
- coach reservations
- flight bookings
- insurance
- local excursions

why not prepare a chart indicating how many agencies provide all of these services, how many only a few and how many only *one*. Discuss the advantages of offering a comprehensive service, and of being a specialist.

You may wish to compile this chart, and to display your findings, during your Application of Number or IT classes, or both.

ATTRACTING CUSTOMERS

Both the leisure and tourism industries are dependent upon *visitors* to make their operation successful. It is difficult to decide what motivates someone to visit one attraction rather than another. Visitor attractions tend to retain popularity for a number of years, then suffer a decline and then pick up again. One factor which will influence client choice is *novelty*. The first year Buckingham Palace opened to the public, it attracted 377,000 visitors over a period of 56 days, which is roughly equivalent to Wembley Stadium filled to capacity five times. That year obviously presented more of a challenge for *other* visitor attractions that may otherwise have drawn in those customers.

Table 1.1 Top 20 attractions charging admission in 1992

Ranking	Attraction	Thousands
1	Alton Towers, Staffordshire	2,501
2	Madame Tussaud's, London	2,264
3	Tower of London	2,235
4	Natural History Museum, London	1,700
5	St Paul's Cathedral, London	1,400
6	Tower World, Blackpool	1,300
7	Science Museum, London	1,213
8	Chessington World of Adventures	1,170
9	Thorpe Park, Surrey	1,026
10	Royal Academy, London	1,018
11	Flamingo Land, North Yorkshire	991
12	Edinburgh Castle	986
13	Kew Gardens	953
14	Drayton Manor Park, Staffordshire	950
15	London Zoo	940
16	Roman Baths and Pump Room, Bath	896
17	American Adventure, Ilkeston	860
18	Jorvik Viking Centre, York	785
19	Windsor Castle, State Apartments	769
20	Chester Zoo	768

Source: British Tourist Authority leaflet, 'National Facts of Tourism', November, 1993.

Thankfully, not all the attractions listed in Table 1.1 are chasing the same people, since different facilities appeal to different sections of the population.

Figure 1.5 A promotional leaflet for Madame Tussaud's.

The population can be divided in many ways. The most obvious divisions are:

i Young–Old
ii Male–Female
iii Active–Passive

It is also important to take into account a number of *social* factors. Certain groups that have special needs may include:

- the unemployed
- the physically disabled
- the mentally disabled
- certain ethnic minorities

and many more.

activity

1 In pairs, make a list of the problems likely to be encountered by *three* of these groups when accessing either a tourism or leisure facility. Then list other groups which could be added to the list.

2 Which of the following groups of customers listed a–d would be *most* likely to use or visit the facilities listed i–iv?

a young women
b overseas visitors
c young men
d families

i Hampton Court
ii a theme park
iii water aerobics
iv snooker

3 Which of the following holidays i–iv would be *most* likely to attract the groups a–d?

i an adventure camp
ii a holiday camp
iii rock climbing
iv a coach tour

a the elderly
b young people
c a youth group
d families

We must now add another important factor to our list of things which influence the customer demand for and interest in a facility or event. The *price* of many tourist attractions may be very high, but visitors continue to increase in numbers every year.

activity

1 Complete Table 1.2 opposite – in particular, the current prices for adults. Add two similar attractions in your locality, showing *their* current prices. How do these prices compare with those for the attractions listed? You may wish to check if there are any subsidies for:

- the unemployed
- senior citizens
- children
- groups

2 Having compared costs for certain attractions, now compare the respective national and local prices for:

i a ticket for an England match at Wembley Stadium and a ticket for a match at your local football club
ii ice-skating at an international venue and ice-skating at a local rink
iii joining a golf club with an international clientele televised for competitions, and joining a local golf club.

You may wish to calculate the revenue for a particular sport/club and compare nationally and locally. Overheads, the cost of players and the location all contribute. Are there marked differences, and if so, can you see *why*?

Table 1.2

	Location	Admission price	Daily opening times	Seasonal opening times
The Tower of London				
Alton Towers				
Dan-yr-Ogof Caves				

The leisure and tourism industries were derived from the need to provide individuals and groups with entertainment, safe and secure travel, and accommodation away from home. They are made up of a combination of products and services which include a range of different employment opportunities.

People spend time away from home for a wide variety of reasons – for example, for business reasons, in which case they will stay in a hotel.

activity

Discuss the different reasons why people travel away from home. List three different reasons for travelling, and give examples of where people may stay.

Business travel is an important part of the travel and tourism industry, especially as business means different things to different people. In the USA, 2 million people travel each year on state affairs alone, and they account for 69 per cent of domestic business travel. Those who travel for business will have different needs from those who travel for leisure or pleasure. Business travellers want a fast, efficient and comfortable journey, with a hotel that can provide quality service and that includes many of the facilities they would expect to find in their office. Price is often not the main consideration.

Tourists, by contrast, will put up with lower-quality service when they travel, especially if their destination is overseas. Group travel often involves charter flights, and these are often subject to delay. Airports are crowded, and flights occur at inconvenient times, but if they are reasonably priced they are acceptable. The destination accommodation can be wide-ranging, from luxury villas to camp sites, but it is generally located near to a range of activities and plenty of restaurants and bars, and it usually provides an information service, some local tours and foreign-exchange facilities.

activity

The following are examples of national or international companies within the leisure and tourism industries:

- Thomas Cook
- First Leisure
- First Choice
- Butlins
- Mecca
- Hilton
- Whitbread
- Radisson Edwardian Hotels
- Stakis

1 For each of the above organisations, which sector are they mainly concerned with?
2 For each again, name three different towns or cities where there is a branch.
3 Which of these organisations have branches within your locality? If you do not have any of the above

organisations near you, or if you require further information, you should write to the head office to request a corporate brochure. (A corporate brochure is a company brochure which lists the full addresses and telephone and fax numbers of all the company's branches.)

4 By way of classroom exercise, you could make comparisons as to the size and locations of the above organisations.

Every country has a combination of outgoing and incoming tourist traffic, and this is acknowledged as a major earner of foreign-currency revenue. The earning power of the tourism industry is indeed one of its positive points, both in the UK and in many other countries. This fact, along with tourism's status as a major employer, means that the creation of a new facility would have a very positive economic impact on any region. However, it is not all good news. The creation of any new facility means demolition or the loss of green space, and while some people prosper, others will suffer or will be disadvantaged.

activity

Discuss the issues as a group before completing the self-assessment question at the end of this unit.

activity

So far we have looked at the needs of clients who *use* a facility. However, there are many clients who wish not to participate but to *spectate*, and they too are an important source of business: Twickenham, for example, can hold 76,000 spectators for an international match and may employ up to 1,000 staff for one event, and all for 15 players. So it is important to realise that leisure is not only about activity but also about watching. Even tourism is, to a certain extent, a spectator activity – e.g. the Changing of the Guard, Trooping the Colour, annual village parades and events.

If you were planning to go to a rock concert which is 100 miles away from home, what would you need:

i on arrival
ii during the day and the event
iii after the event

in order to make sure your day is as enjoyable as possible?

Preparing for employment in the leisure and tourism industries

Strictly speaking, there is no such thing as the 'leisure and tourism industry'. More accurately, the term is like an umbrella which shelters lots of different operations and activities. If you are thinking of a career in leisure and tourism, you could be aiming to work in any of the following areas or contexts:

- travel and tourism
- leisure
- accommodation
- hotel and catering
- arts and heritage
- entertainment
- education

Within each of these areas there are many different jobs available, at all levels. There are opportunities for those

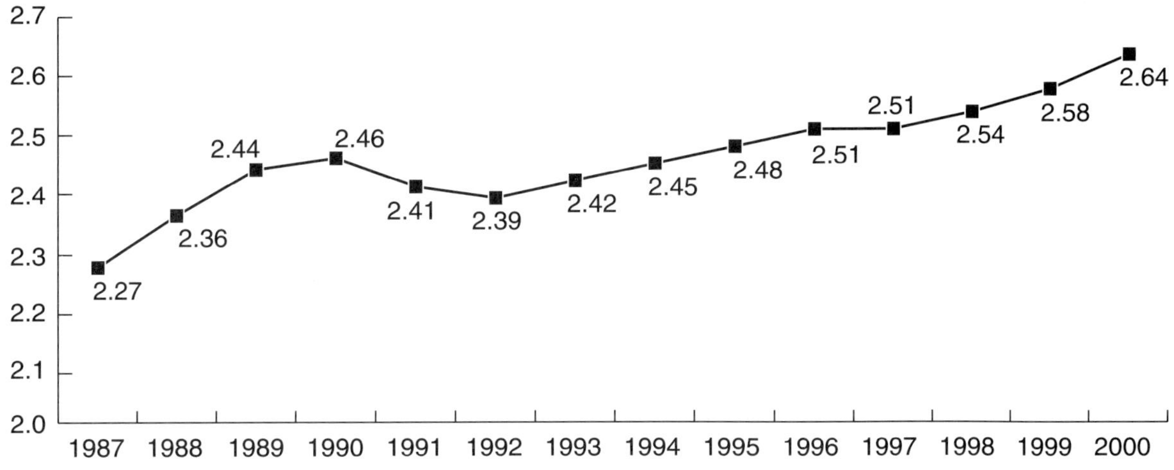

Annual % change — *Forecast*

1988	**1989**	**1990**	**1991**	**1992**	**1993**	**1994**	**1995**	**1996**	**1997**	**1998**	**1999**	**2000**
4.0	3.3	0.9	–2.0	–0.8	1.3	1.2	1.2	1.2	0	1.2	1.6	2.3

Source: Department of Employment (1987–92)

Figure 1.6 Total employment in the hotel and catering industry 1987–2000 (millions).

who want to start at the bottom and work their way up, taking qualifications as they go, and there are managerial opportunities for those who wish to enter direct from university or from a responsible position in an associated industry.

Taken as a whole, the leisure and tourism industry is the largest single employer in the UK, and the range of jobs on offer is enormous. The following directory should give you an idea of the size of the industry you are about to start working in.

DIRECTORY OF JOBS AND AREAS OF EMPLOYMENT IN THE LEISURE AND TOURISM INDUSTRIES

Accommodation Manager
Airline Steward/ess
Airline Reservations Clerk
Account Clerk

Courier
Cashier
Customer Services
Conference Organiser
Cruise Lines Operative
Curator

Domestic Services Manager
Domestic Bursar

Front Office Manager

Ground Steward/ess
Guesthouse Owner/Manager
Guest Services
Guides

Heritage Centre
Holiday Camp
Hotel Booking Agency
Hotel Manager
Housekeeper
Hotel Management

Leisure Centre Manager
Leisure Centre Operatives
Linenkeeper
Lifeguard

Management Trainee

Public Relations Officer

Receptionist
Redcoat (Entertainment Officer)
Reservations Clerk

Reservations Manager
Recreation Centre Staff
Resort Representative
Room Maid

Sales and Marketing
Sports Centre Staff

Theme Park Staff
Tour Operator
Tour Representative
Tourist Boards
Travel Agents

activity

In small groups, or as a class, try to add at least another 20 jobs to the directory.

The job roles in the directory involve a degree of overlap. For example, many of the tasks performed by a travel agent are similar to those performed by a hotel receptionist:

- answering the phone
- dealing with clients
- making bookings
- confirming invoices
- taking payments

Indeed it is quite fair to say that there is on the whole a lot of overlap both between jobs and between different employment contexts in this industry. This is good for us because it means that we can be flexible and that there are increased employment and career opportunities.

activity

Divide into groups and go through a section of the directory each, stating which context each job in that section would be found in. (Some jobs may appear in more than one context.) Collate your information, and convert the totals for each context into a percentage.

Produce a pie chart showing employment opportunities within the leisure and tourism industry.

Note: You may wish to do part of this assignment in Key Skills.

Fortunately we are all different people, with different strengths and weaknesses. In every college group, for example, there will always be one person who:

i always has an answer, or
ii is never late, or
iii never does any homework, or
iv always gets good marks.

There are many other characteristics which you can add, and without a doubt, no one person will have them all.

activity

Make a list of your own strengths and weaknesses for a job in the leisure and tourism industry. Be honest, and ask a friend or your tutor to check it.

Let us consider two different jobs offered by a *tour operator* (who employs a variety of different personnel):

1 A *rep* will need to be lively, with a good personality and sympathetic, organised, capable of working alone or on their own initiative, and perhaps able to offer first aid and another language as skills.
2 A *reservation clerk* employed by the same company will need a good telephone manner, to be efficient, neat and literate, always to be relied upon to work as part of a team, and perhaps able to offer skills in word processing or IT.

Many things will influence your ability to gain a particular job, or to do it well.

activity

Before reading on, make a list of all the things that you think are important when applying for a particular job.

Did you include the following?

- personal presentation
- attitude
- qualifications
- skills
- experience

activity

Discuss ways in which each of the above could be improved, *or* discuss why each of the above is important.

JOB EXAMPLE: RECEPTIONIST

One job we have already mentioned is that of a receptionist. A receptionist would be able to transfer from one context to another, or to move up the ladder with increased experience. Any of the following areas would provide work for a receptionist:

- hotels
- airports
- leisure centres
- car hire
- garages
- doctors'/dentists' surgeries
- hair/beauty salons
- banks
- business houses

Many receptionists enjoy their job so much that they have no wish to move into another type of work. Opportunities for advancement do exist, however, by moving to a large organisation, where a *head receptionist* may control a team of others, or by moving into secretarial or public-relations positions. Others, particularly those who have gained hotel experience, move into the airlines or into tour operations as couriers.

Figure 1.7 Receptionists at work for Cunard Line.

The job of the receptionist will vary according to the type of organisation. In a salon or surgery, it is usual to work alone, while business organisations may employ two or even three staff according to the size of the place and the volume of traffic through the reception area. The job of the *hotel* receptionist is particularly influenced by the type, size and age of the hotel.

By far the biggest employer of reception staff is the hospitality sector. This industry includes not only hotels and motels, but also travel and tourism outlets, and leisure and recreation centres.

RESPONSIBILITIES

Those receptionists who work alone will need to be confident and organised, since the entire workforce in the building depends upon the system of appointments maintained at reception. Different approaches will be needed by those working in the business environment compared with those working in the medical field, while a receptionist in a leisure centre or beauty salon must remember that the clients are there to enjoy themselves.

activity

1 Using the job description for a junior receptionist (right), draw up a job specification using the headings provided. Perhaps you could think of other qualities required.
2 Before reading on, try to make a list of those tasks common to all receptionists.

Your list probably included all of the following:

- appointments/booking
- telephone duties
- face-to-face client contact
- record keeping
- clerical work
- accounts
- cash handling

Did you also think to include the importance of selling the product (as in hotels) and making a profit?

Activities like the one above should make it possible for each individual to evaluate their *own* skills against those required.

Some people enjoy the responsibility of working alone, while others, if they are honest, know they need the support of others. This is why a course of study like this is so important. You have time to think about your strong points, and to try to do something about them. By the time you have finished your course, or even *now*, you may know what type of work you would like to do, but be honest in your self-appraisal nonetheless.

WOULD YOU EMPLOY YOURSELF?

The following is an extract from a job description for a junior receptionist from a large London hotel.

JOB TITLE:	**RECEPTIONIST/CASHIER**
DEPARTMENT:	**RECEPTION**
RESPONSIBLE TO:	**SHIFT LEADER/FRONT OF HOUSE MANAGER**
RESPONSIBLE FOR:	**N/A**

PRIMARY PURPOSE OF THE JOB

TO ENSURE THAT GUESTS ARE CHECKED IN AND OUT OF THE HOTEL IN ACCORDANCE TO COMPANY STANDARDS. TO ENSURE THAT ALL THE NEEDS OF THE CUSTOMER ARE MET AND EXCEEDED IN A FRIENDLY AND PROFESSIONAL MANNER. TO BE AWARE AND FOLLOW ALL ACCOUNTS PROCEDURES CORRECTLY AND TO ENSURE THAT YOUR CASH FLOAT IS CORRECT AT ALL TIMES.

SUMMARIES OF DUTIES AND RESPONSIBILITIES

RECEPTION/CASHIER

- To welcome all customers to the hotel to the standard required.
- To check-in and check-out customers to the standard required.
- To ensure that the payment method is verified upon check-in and follow each different payment type to the standard required.
- To ensure that the registration card is completed to the standard required covering legal responsibilities.
- To ensure that all cash transactions and banking are carried out to the company standard.
- To ensure that all shifts are closed and balanced to the company standard.
- To ensure that all rates are correct based on the published rates and that confidential rates are not submitted to the customer.
- To perform all corrections, refunds and paid-outs in accordance with company procedure.
- To be fully conversant with the computer software.
- To be aware of house counts and availability when taking reversations.
- To take reservations to the standard required.
- To check the credit limit report daily and follow up on all outstanding balances.
- To charge car park and coach services according to company policy.
- To answer the telephone to the standard required.

- To deal with guest complaints to the standard required.
- To liaise with other departments when necessary.
- To pay in monies from other departments to the standard required.

SWITCHBOARD

- To answer telephone calls to the standard required.
- To be aware of bomb threat procedures.
- To log and give wake-up calls to the standard required.
- To know how to operate the voice mail system and the message system.
- To be able to log and send faxes, and to be able to receive and process incoming faxes.
- To be conversant with the bleep system and procedures.
- To familiarise yourself with the Internal telephone list.
- To be able to bar and open telephone lines according to company policy.

CUSTOMER SERVICES

- To accompany all guests to rooms to the standard procedure.
- To explain guest facilities in the room.
- To encourage in-house sales, i.e. restaurant.
- To encourage use of express check-outs for customers other than those paying cash.
- To attend to guests' needs in the lobby.

GENERAL

- Be aware of all Health and Safety Regulations regarding your department.
- To attend all training sessions as required.
- To adhere to all emergency procedures e.g., fire and bomb.

This job description cannot be exhaustive due to the peculiar nature of the hotel industry; the job holder may be required to carry out tasks as specified by Management.

This job description is sent out with every application form so that the applicant knows what is expected of them. The hotel will use the job description to construct a job or person specification which tells them what type of person they want to do the job. The requirements are usually listed under different headings, such as Qualifications, Experience and Special Aptitudes, and a note is made under each heading as to whether each requirement is essential or desirable.

All jobs will be shortlisted in the same sort of way, so even if you have no interest at all in reception/ administration jobs, or no interest in the hotel sector, remember that they all fall under the leisure and tourism umbrella, and that the employer that you do choose will have similar standards and values to all other employers in the industry.

Make sure also that the employer you choose *chooses you*.

QUALIFICATIONS

Some qualifications are 'generic' to our industry, in other words they can be used across all contexts under the umbrella of 'leisure and tourism'. One way of picturing this is by means of the pyramid shown in Figure 1.8 on page 18. The qualifications get harder the further up you go.

Other qualifications, on the other hand, are 'specific' or vocational, and are essential for various specific jobs. For example, a lifeguard *may* have a GNVQ Intermediate/ Advanced or a B/TEC National, but they *must* have a Pool Bronze.

It is useful, therefore, to put together a selection of qualifications and skills which will help you in your chosen job.

activity

1 How many steps would it take to reach the position of Owner/ Manager shown in Figure 1.9 on page 18? What qualifications will you need to gain on the way?

2 Identify and describe qualifications, skills and experience required for suitable job roles in

one particular sector within the leisure and tourism industry. Describe how to acquire them.

3 Promotion in any industry is by a series of steps, hence the expression 'further up the ladder'. Those who are ambitious will climb to the top of the ladder, while others are happy to remain on the lower steps or halfway up. Consider the 'ladder' of jobs available in the leisure sector.

activity

Research the appropriate specific qualifications for a job of your choice. Find out how the qualifications can be obtained, how long they take and how much they will cost.

Make a brief presentation to the class, to include any necessary previous qualifications required and any cost advantages which can be gained through group participation in the qualifications.

Qualifications can be gained in a variety of ways, including full-time (such as GNVQ) where it is often possible to include an additional course of study (such as first aid or a European language). Other qualifications are on offer on a part-time basis – either one day a week or one evening a week – and others still, mainly NVQs, can be gained while you are actually doing the job: as you learn, you will be accredited with units to give you your

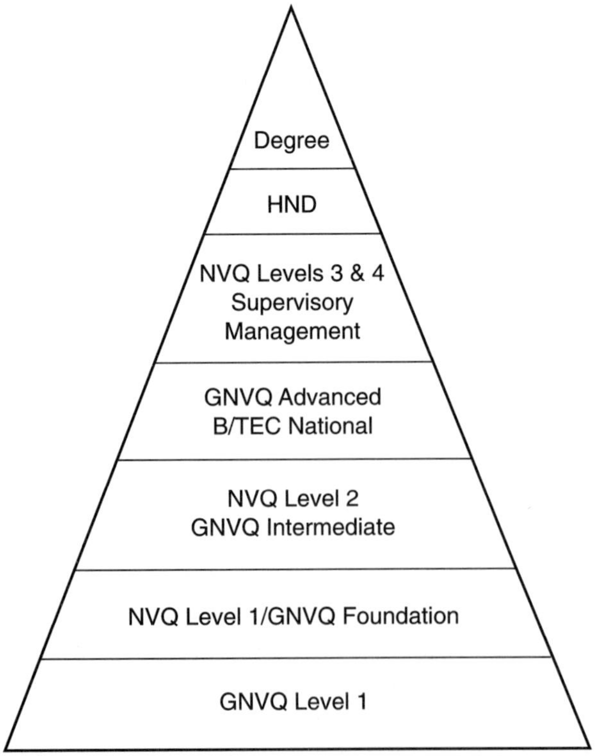

Figure 1.8 Pyramid of generic qualifications.

Figure 1.9 Your career ladder.

qualification. Other organisations produce their own training programme, and while they may not award an NVQ, they will have a company award, much of which will be transferable if you move to another organisation.

Skills and experience are also often gained from work experience or various forms of *job shadowing*, and while this may not result in a qualification, it is always useful experience which you can quote when applying for a job. If you have worked well, you may be given a reference, and this is another useful aid which can be included in your application.

Some courses are residential, or highly intensive, and the qualification is obtained all in one go at the end of the course. This is useful, because it enables you to concentrate on the job in hand, but it is difficult sometimes if you have other commitments also. Other courses and qualifications are offered through open or flexible learning. This is useful if you are already working and, because of shifts, find it hard to attend evening classes. This is, however, a hard way to study because you need to be very well motivated to succeed in studying for qualifications alone.

activity

List one example of qualifications in leisure and tourism which can be obtained by each of the methods mentioned above.

THE JOB SEARCH

THE CV

Compiling a *curriculum vitae* (an outline of your educational and work history) is one of the most important tasks you will undertake, and it is essential to include all the relevant information about yourself and your qualifications. Your CV has to sell you and your qualities to a prospective employer, and even if you are the most suitable applicant for the job, if your CV is not presentable and easy to read, then you may not get called for an interview. Some people have their CVs professionally compiled and presented in a folder, but if you follow a few simple guidelines, it is possible to produce an acceptable CV by using a typewriter, word processor or computer.

activity

Using the skeleton CV shown in Table 1.3 on page 20; prepare a CV which you feel accurately reflects you and your qualities. (It is never too early to have a CV!) If possible, use a computer and save on disk: you then only have to upgrade the information as and when required. See if you can do this in your IT class.

It is obviously very important to have the *right* qualifications on your CV for the job, but it is just as important that the employer can see your qualifications and skills *at a glance*. There are many different ways to present a CV, and you should begin work on it whilst still studying; it can then be added to when you change jobs, gain further work experience or undertake further education.

THE NATURE AND SCOPE OF THE WORK

Luckily for all of us, leisure and tourism continues to be a growth industry with plenty of employment opportunities. By now you will have realised that most jobs in this industry include:

i dealing with people
ii some paper work
iii some figure work.

Many jobs also involve shift work – including working over evenings and weekends – and some jobs will take you away from home. If you see these things as a disadvantage (although to many employees they are the *attraction*), on the positive side you can count on a career which provides you with a wide variety of skills, most of which are transferable: if you decide you would like to move to another section of the industry, you may indeed find that you are already suitably qualified.

Table 1.3 A skeleton CV

CURRICULUM VITAE

Name:

Address:

Telephone:

Date of birth: [date, month, year]

Marital status: [single/married]

EDUCATION

Schools attended

19__ to 19__ [insert years]: [name of school(s), full postal address of school(s)]

Qualifications gained

[list here all the subjects passed, level of achievement and grade where necessary]

Further education

Colleges attended

19__ to 19__ [insert years]: [name of school or college, full postal address of school or college]

Qualifications gained

[list here all the subjects studied, the board of examination (e.g. City & Guilds) and the level of achievement or grade]

Other training/education

[list here any other training/education, with names/addresses of any relevant establishments]

WORK EXPERIENCE

_______ 19__ to _______ 19__ [insert months and years]: [name and address of establishment]

Duties included

[state all necessary information about the post]

_______ 19__ to _______ 19__ [insert months and years]: [name and address of establishment]

Duties included

[state all necessary information about the post]

Industry-related experience

_______ 19__ to _______ 19__ [insert months and years]: [name and address of establishment]

Duties included

[state all necessary information about the post]

[NB: include any part-time work experience]

WORK HISTORY

_______ 19__ to _______ 19__ [insert months and years]: [name and address of establishment]

Duties included

[state all necessary information about the post]

_______ 19__ to _______ 19__ [insert months and years]: [name and address of establishment]

Duties included

[state all necessary information about the post]

OTHER INFORMATION

[list here any other information you feel necessary, including school achievements (other than exams), nominations for awards, recognition for good work, driving licence etc.]

HOBBIES/INTERESTS

[list here all hobbies/interests/pastimes you have]

activity

Using the following headings, make a list of jobs by consulting relevant trade publications and the local/national press:

- tourism
- hotels
- leisure
- sports/recreation
- arts
- entertainment

Maybe you found that some sectors in the activity seem to have a wider variety of jobs than others. This is quite true, and if you consult Table 1.4 on hotel and catering employment, you will see some interesting figures.

APPLICATIONS AND INTERVIEWS

Job vacancies may be found in a variety of different ways:

i by word of mouth – a friend or relative telling you of a vacancy
ii in a local or national newspaper
iii at a Job Centre
iv through a private employment agency

Table 1.4 Comparison of estimates of hotel and catering employment for 1987 and 1990 (thousands)

	1991 estimates (used in previous report[1])			1992 estimates (used in this report)		
	1987	1990	Change 1987–90	1987	1990	Change 1987–90
Restaurants	237	281	44	238	306	68
Pubs	263	286	23	265	339	74
Clubs	140	145	5	140	143	3
Contract catering	121	131	10	101	122	22
Hotels (including holiday camps)	250	281	31	251	303	52
Self employed	200	162	−38	184	167	−17
Commercial sectors	1,211	1,286	75	1,178	1,380	202
Recreation and culture	29	33	4	29	33	4
Travel	24	21	−3	24	20	−4
Retail	46	49	3	46	45	−1
Industrial[2]	256	246	−10	256	240	−16
Education	264	281	17	264	279	15
Medical	348	333	−15	348	321	−27
Public administration	45	43	−2	45	43	−2
Personal	81	100	19	81	100	19
Catering-services sectors	1,093	1,106	13	1,093	1,081	−12
Total industry	2,304	2,392	88	2,271	2,461	190

[1] *Meeting Competence Needs*, HCIMA Yearbook
[2] Catering for staff in private-sector industrial and commercial enterprises

v in trade or specialist magazines, e.g. *Caterer and Hotelkeeper*, *Travel Trade Gazette*, *Leisure Management*
vi on local radio.

If you find a position for which you feel you are qualified and which interests you, there will be instructions as to how to apply:

i telephone for an application form, or
ii telephone for further details, or
iii maybe just an address is given, which indicates that you must write a letter of application – and you could also send a copy of your CV for their consideration.

activity

As a group, obtain copies of both a local newspaper and a specialist leisure and tourism magazine. Find a job which you would like to apply for when you finish college.

1 Write a letter of application.
2 Compile a CV.

You may then wish to take this a stage further. Get other members of your group to read your letter of application and CV, and read theirs in turn. Your lecturer may agree to conduct mock interviews with you to assess your suitability, and if you have the facilities, you may wish to video the interview and then suggest any good or bad points and areas for improvement. It is a good idea to practise interviews beforehand, as they can be very nerve-racking.

If you apply for a position, you may be sent an application form. If this is the case, either make a copy and complete the copy before transferring your details onto the original application form, or complete the original form in pencil: it is then easy to check for mistakes and make alterations without spoiling the original form. Read any instructions carefully: are you required to print in block capitals, or do you have to handwrite the form? If you have been asked to provide a referee on the form, be sure to ask the person in advance to make sure they will agree to this.

activity

Complete the application form shown in Figure 1.10 on pages 24–7. Ask your lecturer to check the form for any errors, changes etc.

If you are invited for an interview, make sure you know exactly where the interview is being held and how long it will take to get there. You may wish to travel to the organisation *before* the interview date in order to time the journey. Don't arrive late; and remember, if you are kept waiting, you will have the advantage as they will begin by apologising to you. Make sure also that you are suitably dressed – this is not an outing with your friends or a fashion show! And finally, if you have them, take with you the following:

i copies of certificates
ii a record of your achievements
iii references
iv awards.

You may see positions advertised both locally and nationally, but if you have a clear idea of what you are looking for, or perhaps require information as part of research or assignment work for your course, you may wish to refer to the directory of organisations and associations that follows on pages 28–9.

WHERE DID YOU HEAR ABOUT THIS VACANCY?:

....

Radisson Edwardian
HOTELS LONDON

JOB APPLICATION FORM

POSITION APPLIED FOR: ______________________

Please state: Full Time, Part Time or Casual: ______________________

Photograph if available

PERSONAL DETAILS

SURNAME:.. FORENAMES:..

TITLE (MR/MRS/MISS/MS):...................................... DATE OF BIRTH:..

HOME ADDRESS:..

....

HOME TELEPHONE:... WORK TELEPHONE:...

CONTACT IN CASE OF EMERGENCY: NAME:..

RELATIONSHIP:... TELEPHONE NUMBER:...

ADDRESS:..

DO YOU HOLD A CURRENT UK DRIVING LICENSE? YES/NO TYPE:............................ NO OF ENDORSEMENTS/POINTS:............................

ARE YOU REGISTERED DISABLED: YES/NO NUMBER: ....

DO YOU HOLD A FIRST AID CERTIFICATE? YES/NO NUMBER:..

HAVE YOU BEEN CONVICTED OF A CRIMINAL OFFENCE OR HAVE YOU ANY CHARGES OUTSTANDING?

YES/NO (If 'Yes' - please give details below)

....

....

(Convictions defined as 'SPENT' under the Rehabilitation of Offenders Act should not be mentioned)

NATIONALITY:..

DO YOU REQUIRE A WORK PERMIT TO WORK IN THE UK? YES/NO
(If unsure, please ask your Interviewer)

IF SO PLEASE PROVIDE PROOF OF PERMIT WITH APPLICATION

HOBBIES AND INTERESTS: ....

....

....

Figure 1.10 A general application form for Radisson Edwardian Hotels.

EDUCATION AND TRAINING

SECONDARY EDUCATION (OR MOST RECENT SCHOOLING)	DATES FROM TO	SUBJECT/LEVEL	GRADE

FURTHER EDUCATION COLLEGE/UNIVERSITY	DATES FROM TO	COURSES/SUBJECT	GRADE

OTHER COURSES ATTENDED	DURATION	SUBJECT

MEMBERSHIP OF ANY PROFESSIONAL BODIES:..........

....

....

PRESENT EMPLOYMENT

NAME OF CURRENT/LAST EMPLOYER:..........

ADDRESS:..........

JOB TITLE:.......... WAGE:.......... REASON FOR LEAVING:..........

DATE COMMENCED:.......... DATE FINISHED/AMOUNT OF NOTICE REQ:..........

MAY WE APPLY FOR REFERENCES NOW?: YES/NO

Main Duties & Responsibilities:

....

....

....

....

....

....

Figure 1.10 continued.

PREVIOUS EMPLOYMENT
(Can be carried on over the page if more space is needed. Unless stated not to, we will apply for references.)
STARTING WITH MOST RECENT:

NAME & ADDRESS OF EMPLOYER	DATES From & To	REASON FOR LEAVING	POSITION HELD & MAIN RESPONSIBILITIES
NAME & ADDRESS OF EMPLOYER	DATES From & To	REASON FOR LEAVING	POSITION HELD & MAIN RESPONSIBILITIES
NAME & ADDRESS OF EMPLOYER	DATES From & To	REASON FOR LEAVING	POSITION HELD & MAIN RESPONSIBILITIES

DO YOU SPEAK ANY LANGUAGES OTHER THAN ENGLISH? (Please List):

....

....

PLEASE GIVE ANY OTHER INFORMATION THAT YOU FEEL MAY SUPPORT YOUR APPLICATION (eg Technical Skills such as Work Processing, Book-keeping, Typing etc or Personal/Character Qualities)

....

....

DECLARATION: I certify that the information given is to the best of my knowledge, complete and accurate and I understand that if any statement is subsequently found to be false or misleading my employment may be terminated.

SIGNED:.. DATE:...

It is company policy to take up employment and personal references on all staff covering the past 3 years minimum, and any offer of employment is made subject to the satisfactory completion of this process. Company addresses and reference contacts must be provided covering at least 3 years in current and past employment employers details. Please provide any further information you feel is relevant to your application for employment on a separate sheet.

Figure 1.10 continued.

Radisson Edwardian
HOTELS LONDON

EMPLOYEE HEALTH QUESTIONNAIRE

EMPLOYEE NAME..

HOTEL...

POSITION..

NAME & ADDRESS OF EMPLOYEE'S DOCTOR...
....
....
....
....

Please circle "Yes" or "No" for the following questions:-

(1) Have you within the past 3 years had any illness or accident which caused you to be off work for 2 weeks or more ? **YES / NO**

(2) If yes, what was the illness or accident
....
....
....

(3) Have you within the past 3 years attended an out-patients clinic or had a course of treatment (tablets, injections, or physiotherapy) lasting one month or more ? **YES / NO**

(4) Are you receiving any such treatment ? **YES / NO**

(5) Are you suffering from, or have you suffered from, one or more of the following:-

* Fits, epilepsy or blackouts **YES / NO**
* Diabetes **YES / NO**
* Depressive illness or nervous trouble **YES / NO**
* Bowel trouble (eg; typhoid or recurring diarrhoea) **YES / NO**
* Skin disease or dermatitis **YES / NO**
* Allergy (to any drugs or to handling any substances) **YES / NO**
* Earache or ear infection **YES / NO**

(6) Are you on the Disabled Register ? **YES / NO**

(7) If yes, what is your number ....
what is the expiry date ....
what is the disablement.......................................

SIGNATURE OF EMPLOYEE...

DATE..

Figure 1.10 continued.

DIRECTORY OF ASSOCIATIONS AND ORGANISATIONS

Association of British Travel Agents (ABTA)
55–57 Newman St
London W1P 4AH
Tel.: 0171 637 2444
Fax: 0171 637 0713

Association of Conferences and Events (ACE International)
Riverside House
High St
Huntingdon
Cambs PE18 6SG
Tel.: 01480 457595
Fax: 01480 412963

Association of Exhibition Organisers
26 Chapter St
London SWIP 4ND
Tel.: 0171 932 0252
Fax: 0171 932 0299

Association of Teachers of Tourism
c/o Tourism Society
26 Chapter St
London SW1P 4ND
Tel.: 0171 834 0461
Fax: 0171 932 0238

Automobile Association
Fanum House
Basingstoke
Hants RG21 2EA
Tel.: 01256 20123
Fax: 01256 493389

British Association of Conference Towns
1st Floor
Elizabeth House
22 Suffolk St
Queensway
Birmingham B1 1LS
Tel.: 0121 616 1400
Fax: 0121 616 1364

British Association of Tourism Officers
PO Box 547
Brighton BN1 6WW
Tel.: 01273 550523
Fax: 01273 550523

British Federation of Hotel, Guest House and Self Catering Associations
5 Sandicroft Rd
Blackpool
Lancs FY1 2RY
Tel.: 01253 352683

British Hospitality Association
40 Duke St
London W1M 6HR
Tel.: 0171 499 6641

British Incoming Tour Operators Association
Vigilant House
120 Wilton Rd
London SW1V 1JZ
Tel.: 0171 931 0601

British Institute of Facilities Management
67 High St
Saffron Walden
Essex CB10 1AA
Tel.: 01799 508608

British Institute of Innkeeping
Wessex House
80 Park St
Camberley
Surrey GU15 3PT
Tel.: 01276 684449

British Resorts Association
8 Post Office Ave
Southport
Lancs PR9 0US
Tel.: 0151 934 2286
Fax: 0151 934 2287

British Safety Council
70 Chancellors Rd
London W6 9RS
Tel.: 0181 741 1231
Fax: 0181 741 4555

British Spas Federation
Westfield
Hallow
Worcester WR2 6LB
Tel.: 01905 640202
Fax: 01905 640202

British Standards Institution (BSI)
389 Chiswick High Rd
London W4 4AL
Tel.: 0181 996 9000
Fax: 0181 996 7400
Customer Info: 0908 226888

British Tourist Authority
Thames Tower
Blacks Rd
London W6 9EL
Tel.: 0181 846 9000
Fax: 0181 563 0302

020 8563 3182

Business & Technology Education Council (BTEC)
Central House
Upper Woburn Place
London WC1H 0HH
Tel.: 0171 431 8400
Fax: 0171 387 6068

Camping & Outdoor Leisure Association
58 Station Approach
South Ruislip
Middx HA4 6SA
Tel.: 0181 842 1111
Fax: 0181 842 0090

The Chartered Institute of Marketing
Moor Hall
Cookham
Maidenhead
Berks SL6 9QH
Tel.: 01628 524922
Fax: 01628 531382

City & Guilds of London Institute
1 Giltspur St
London EC1A 9DD
Tel.: 0171 278 2468
Fax: 0171 278 9460

Confederation of British Industry (CBI)
Centre Point
103 New Oxford St
London WC1A 1DU
Tel.: 0171 379 7400
Fax: 0171 240 1578

Confederation of Tourism, Hotel & Catering Management
204 Barnett Wood Lane
Ashtead
Surrey KT21 2DB
Tel.: 01372 278572
Fax: 01372 277778

ASSIGNMENT

Working in groups of 3–4, conduct a mini-survey of approximately 25 people of approximately the same age and social status (another group at college would be ideal) to find out about their awareness of the local leisure and tourism industries.

1. *Choose a facility in the area: this could be a concert hall, football ground, gym, travel agency or anything similar. Discuss within your group why you have chosen this particular facility – make some brief notes.*

2 Devise a list of questions which might include:

i Do you know the location of ________?
ii Have you ever visited ________?
iii Do you go alone?
iv Have you eaten there?

About 15 questions would be ideal.

3 After consulting with your tutor, produce this list in the form of a questionnaire, with two boxes for each question offering the choice of 'Yes' or 'No' (if you can do this during IT lessons it would look much better).

4 Approach your subjects at a time most convenient for both of you. Try to find somewhere fairly quiet. (Practise on a group member first.) You can begin by saying 'This will take about X minutes of your time.' Use a clipboard and record the results at once. You will need at least two of you for the interview. It may be useful to have a brochure of your facility with you, for this might help to jog people's memory.

5 Keep asking people until you get enough data to form the basis of a survey. If you aimed for 25, try to get that many.

6 Return to base and collate (put together) all your results, ready to be displayed in an easy-to-read format.

UNIT ONE

test YOURSELF

1 A municipal camp site is most likely to belong to the
- ***a*** voluntary sector
- ***b*** private sector
- ***c*** public sector
- ***d*** tourism sector.

2 Match the facilities i–iv with the contexts a–d
- ***i*** ice rink
- ***ii*** museum
- ***iii*** caravan park
- ***iv*** guided tour

- ***a*** catering and hospitality
- ***b*** travel and tourism
- ***c*** arts and entertainment
- ***d*** sports and recreation.

3 A function of the Sports Council is to
- ***a*** monitor local authorities
- ***b*** enforce current legislation
- ***c*** promote a general understanding of sport
- ***d*** ensure that sport is a part of the school curriculum.

4 The main function of ABTA is to
- ***a*** book overseas holidays
- ***b*** monitor the quality of resorts
- ***c*** ensure that airlines do not overbook
- ***d*** act as arbitrator in cases of disputes.

5 The Arts Council was formed to
- ***a*** enable young artists to study
- ***b*** give grants to galleries
- ***c*** develop and improve public knowledge of the arts
- ***d*** ensure that art is a part of the school curriculum.

6 A youth hostel is generally used for
- ***a*** young people living away from home
- ***b*** young people's holidays
- ***c*** overnight stays for members
- ***d*** pre-booked holidays for members.

7 A travel lodge is most often used for
- ***a*** business travel
- ***b*** tourist travel
- ***c*** conference business
- ***d*** travel agencies.

8 Voluntary organisations are expected to
- ***a*** make a profit every year
- ***b*** show a yearly increase in funds
- ***c*** work for charities overseas
- ***d*** fulfil a need in the community.

9 Accommodation availability in a town can usually be obtained from
- ***a*** ABTA
- ***b*** a tourist information centre
- ***c*** the local tourist board
- ***d*** a travel agent.

10 If a tour operator books car hire for a client, the *principal* is the
- ***a*** tour operator
- ***b*** car hire company
- ***c*** client
- ***d*** travel agent.

11 A CV is a
- ***a*** summary of an individual's strengths
- ***b*** list of attributes needed for a job
- ***c*** description of a job
- ***d*** summary of a company's organisation.

12 A positive economic impact of tourism is
- ***a*** an increase in local amenities
- ***b*** increased employment opportunities
- ***c*** that more people can go abroad
- ***d*** greater environmental awareness.

13 Which of the following leisure activities is in the voluntary sector?
- ***a*** scuba diving
- ***b*** Beavers
- ***c*** snooker halls
- ***d*** skating.

14 Which of the following is most likely to be part of an international organisation?
- ***a*** a travel agent
- ***b*** a leisure centre
- ***c*** a hotel
- ***d*** a tour operator.

15 Which of the following is most likely to be under local-authority control?
- ***a*** a theme park
- ***b*** a tourist information centre
- ***c*** a youth hostel
- ***d*** car parking.

16 Which of the following is most likely to be owned by a national company?
- ***a*** a theatre
- ***b*** a sailing club
- ***c*** a travel agent
- ***d*** a museum.

17 The National Rivers Authority is responsible for
- ***a*** customs checks at main ports
- ***b*** the upkeep of rivers and banks
- ***c*** the safety of all boats
- ***d*** the quality of drinking water.

18 An example of a job which is available in all sectors of the leisure and tourism industry is
- ***a*** courier
- ***b*** recreation assistant
- ***c*** receptionist
- ***d*** accounts clerk.

19 The only world heritage site in England identified by the United Nations is
- ***a*** Stonehenge
- ***b*** the City of Bath
- ***c*** the Tower of London
- ***d*** Sherwood Forest.

20 Travel which is motivated by visiting friends and relations (VFR) is most likely to be profitable to a
- ***a*** hotel
- ***b*** international travel agent
- ***c*** restaurant
- ***d*** motorway service station.

21 List eight examples of venues for arts and entertainment (e.g. theatres).

22 List eight examples of venues for sports and physical activities.

23 Give four examples of providers of travel services.

24 Explain the difference between an internal and an external customer.

CASE STUDY

Wilstead Borough Council has decided to rationalise its facilities for sport and recreation, since many of them are duplicated by private enterprise. Some of the facilities are in a poor state of repair, while others are very costly to upkeep.

The Council has decided upon two courses of action:

1. Certain facilities will be put out to tender, and interested parties will be invited to bid.
2. Other facilities will be sold by auction, which will allow the Council to place a reserve on the property, most of which is freehold.

You are employed at the Woolstaff Inn and Tavern, which has well-established trade with local, passing and repeat business. The Tavern has two large public bars, one saloon which serves bar meals, a games room, a room used for weddings and banquets, a large car park and a children's playground. The owners of the Woolstaff are particularly interested in two of the local-authority properties which border their property. The first is a pitch and putt golf course, the second consists of a number of tennis courts. The pitch and putt will be offered for auction, and the courts (four of them in all) are out to tender. The pitch and putt is in good repair but the cost of upkeep is high, while the tennis courts need some attention: the external wire needs redoing and nets need restringing. There is enough room by the tennis courts to open a small snack bar, and this could also service the pitch and putt.

The owners are particularly keen on these properties since a number of enquiries have been received for weddings and christenings, which they feel could be turned into full weekend sales if there were more leisure facilities available.

1. Find out the difference between tenders and auctions, and either write brief notes on both or give a presentation to the rest of the group.
2. State the advantages and disadvantages of both to the owners of the Woolstaff Inn.
3. If they were successful in gaining both facilities, give ways in which you would promote them:

   i to your regular clients
   ii to past clients
   iii to a new market.

4. Outline a weekend itinerary which you would use to promote a special sporting weekend.
5. Give examples of some services which you could promote as part of the new offer.

unit 2

Marketing and promoting leisure and tourism products

This unit introduces the idea of marketing, and shows how it is used in the leisure and tourism industry as part of our everyday activities.

At the end of this unit, you should have:

I explored the idea of marketing and focused on the important aspect of promotion
II planned a promotional campaign
III run and evaluated the promotional campaign.

Investigating marketing and promotion in leisure and recreation and travel and tourism organisations

It doesn't matter how good an organisation is or how well they have tried to satisfy consumer needs, the public must be aware that they *exist* before they will become successful. Such public awareness can be raised in a number of ways.

activity

State three ways in which an organisation might get customers.

For the above activity, you probably thought of:

i advertising (in all its forms)
ii recommendations
iii opportunity trade.

All forms of advertising are about raising customer awareness, and we shall examine some of these in more detail later. Recommendations, or word of mouth, is one of the best ways of getting customers because it is free, and it also implies that your existing customers are happy. Opportunity trade is often linked to location, but opportunities can also be *sought out* and then turned into sales, and this is what *promotion* is all about.

THE MARKETING FUNCTION

Once customers know about an organisation, they then have to be informed about what it *does*, i.e. what products and services are on offer. However, this task is not the responsibility of the marketing department alone: it is the responsibility of everyone who works in the organisation.

It is in everyone's interests to bring in more and more customers, make profits and thereby make everyone's jobs secure.

Marketing is thus an important part of *all* jobs. But what is it? There have been lots of definitions of marketing, but one of the easiest and most appropriate for us to start with is this: marketing is about getting the right product:

i to the right people
ii at the right price
iii in the right place
iv at the right time.

Consider a product such as a pair of 'designer brand' football boots. The *right people* are easy to identify for this product: young people who play football, either at school or with a club or just for pleasure, or older people who have continued with the sport. The *prices* of this type of product do not vary too much, as long as you are paying for the quality and the name. Obviously, cheaper products are available, but people expect to pay a certain price, especially if the product has been endorsed by a famous footballer. The *right place* is again quite easy to identify. It could be a local sports shop, a specialist section in a department store or a franchise operation in a sports facility. The *right time* in this particular example is the difficult one. Very few people buy football boots between June and August – in fact, you may have difficulty finding *any* purchases during this period. For one thing, boots will not be bought for younger children before the start of the season in case their feet grow. Thus, even if the first four of the above criteria are in place, if you invested a lot of money in football boots in May, you would have to wait a long time to get your money back, because one of the criteria, the *timing*, was wrong.

activity

Other examples of deals which wouldn't work are easy to find. See if you can think of one example for each of the marketing criteria listed which would make successful marketing very difficult. (For example, trying to sell ice creams in the open in Alaska is an instance of either the *wrong product* or the *wrong place*.)

In an industry like ours, marketing is also about another very important factor: satisfying customer needs while still making a profit. *This* is why marketing is *everyone's* responsibility.

THE MARKETING MIX

This is the mix of the actual practical tools of the marketing process, and it describes the way in which they link together. The marketing mix comprises four main parts:

1 price
2 place
3 product
4 promotion.

Figure 2.1 Linford Christie promoting Lucozade.

PRICE

The price is important but not vital. Customers will agree to pay a given price for a variety of reasons.

> ***a c t i v i t y***
>
> Give three factors which affect pricing.

In the above activity, did you include

i value for money
ii location
iii time of day, week, year?

You could also have included: brand name, exclusiveness, market forces, fashion, expectations. From an organisational point of view, pricing may also be affected by government legislation and by unit costs.

PLACE

The place factor is important, but it is also important to remember that a venue may be *moveable*. Although some marketing activities *are* linked to specific locations – e.g. the Changing of the Guard, the Farnborough Airshow, the London Marathon or the FA Cup Final – many events are special, or 'one off', and may be held in fields or marquees, or on boats or planes.

Whatever the place, it needs:

i to be accessible
ii to include some basic facilities
iii to be clean
iv to be secure/safe.

PRODUCT

The product, in leisure and tourism, is really hard to define. It may be something *tangible*, like a pair of trainers or a model of the Tower of London, or it may be a service which is offered to a customer (i.e. something *intangible*), like swimming lessons, a meal or a guided tour. What we are really identifying as a service product is a series of events leading to customer satisfaction. What contributes to this satisfaction could, for example, be:

- the weather
- the night life
- the facilities
- the friendliness

for a *package holiday*, or

- the image
- the quality of the equipment
- the professionalism of the staff

for a *fitness centre*. It is hard to define a service product, and also hard, with this kind of product, to retain customer loyalty, and this is another reason why everyone must be involved. The *tangible* product, on the other hand, such as tickets for a rock concert or sports equipment, is easier to define because it represents an *actual event or physical purchase*.

> ***a c t i v i t y***
>
> Give one example of a product and a service in each of the following contexts:
>
> - hotel
> - restaurant
> - fast-food outlet
> - cinema
> - museum
> - social club
> - coach company
> - airline
> - tourist attraction
> - swimming pool
> - activity centre
> - coaching centre
> - school
> - travel agent
> - taxi
> - ferry operator

When working on the activity above, you may have found that in some cases it is extremely difficult to separate a product from a service. For example, a restaurant obviously provides a service, whether good or bad, but the meal itself is perhaps a product. However, you cannot take it away as you could a bag of shopping (unless you had asked for a doggy bag or takeaway), and even then at some stage the food is eaten. On the other hand, an airline provides both a service – by transporting passengers, providing a meal or looking after the customers' needs – and a product – which may be bought and taken away, e.g. promotional goods, pens, cuddly toys, duty-free gifts, watches and alcohol – and the two here *are* clearly distinguishable.

PROMOTION

Promotional activities are essential to the success of any organisation. Remember, at the beginning of this unit we identified two important ways of promoting:

i word of mouth
ii advertising

In addition, there are a variety of selling techniques:

- personal
- direct mail
- telephone
- sales promotions/campaigns for a specific event

Some companies may employ the services of an advertising agency of a public-relations officer, but very many more rely upon their regular workforce to promote products or services.

MARKET RESEARCH

This describes the activity which gathers together useful information regarding the likes and dislikes of customers (i.e. customer preferences/needs and wants). The best way of getting this information is from the customers themselves, and this can be done in a variety of ways. Getting an opinion from the customers is known as *feedback*, and it should be an ongoing part of market research. If you wanted to arrange a trip to Alton Towers from your school or college, what would you do first?

i Check the price
ii book a suitable date
iii get some coach prices.

All of these are important and are examples of the type of matters people will ask about, but first of all you really need to ask *who* might be interested. In order to find this out, you could compile a questionnaire and circulate it to all the groups you want to target. When the replies come in, this 'sample survey' would give you the feedback you need: i.e. are the groups interested? This kind of feedback is known as *primary data*, and the survey technique involved is sometimes called *field research*. If you were organising a major event or completing a serious survey, you may also wish to know (for example) the names of all the groups who visited Alton Towers *last year* and get some feedback from them. This kind of feedback is known as *secondary data*, and can often be bought from organisations dealing specifically with market research. Research involving this kind of data is known as *desk research*.

Market research is about collecting information. This can be collected in a variety of ways, but it usually comes in the form of a *questionnaire* which:

i informs us about customers
ii gives us their opinion
iii lets them air their views
iv informs us of their habits.

So if we wish to monitor a new product, market research should show us:

i what our customers are like
ii what they think of the product
iii whether they like or dislike the idea of change
iv how often they come

and we can collect any variation on this type of information providing we formulate the questionnaire in such a way that the required information will be received.

Information collected can then be put to many different uses.

THE NATURE OF PRODUCTS

Remember that a product is defined as goods or services, and that we recently distinguished between tangible and intangible products. However, some products are very hard to place in either of these two categories, and for that reason such products may be described as a mixture of tangible and intangible.

The official MRS Identity Card

- If you wish to validate the authenticity of this interview, please ring FREE on:

0500 39 69 99

and ask for Market Research Society

THANK YOU FOR ANSWERING OUR QUESTIONS.

Now we hope we can answer some of yours.

Your interview was carried out by:

On (date):

What is the Market Research Society?

The MRS is the body responsible for professional standards and helps to ensure the following: none of the information gathered for research purposes is ever used for any other purpose, it is confidential, you are guaranteed anonymity and all research is conducted strictly in accordance with the MRS Code of Conduct.

MRS *The Market Research Society*
15 Northburgh Street
London EC1V 0AH

What is market research anyway?

All sorts of organisations want to know what the general public thinks, from government and political parties through to retailers and companies who provide a product or service. They will use the information to guide their policies, product developments and services. The job of the interviewer is to find out, using research like the interview you have just participated in, what people really want.

Why me?

Clearly we can't ask everyone, so we have to ask a representative sample of people of all ages and types.

Why do you want personal details like my name, address and telephone number, especially if it's going to be confidential?

For two reasons.

Firstly we need to make sure we have people from all the relevant age groups, income groups etc, and we can only find that out by asking.

Secondly, as we need to validate interviews in the interests of our clients, it is possible that someone will contact you by phone, letter or in person to check that your interview was conducted properly.

What protection do I have?

The following specific measures are designed to protect you and others:

The Data Protection Act.
All information gathered by us is covered by this Act. It can only be used for statistical or research purposes, you will never receive sales calls or direct mail as a result of giving us your name.

The ID Card.
Carried by most legitimate researchers.

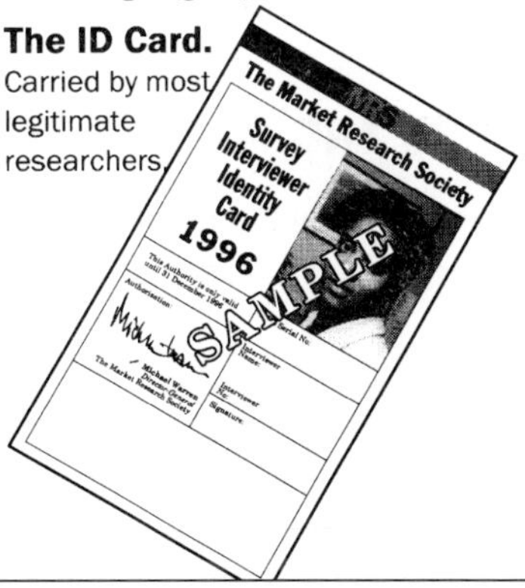

Figure 2.2 This leaflet from the MRS is handed out to all their interviewees and gives details about the process.

activity

Give two examples of products which would fall into this 'mixed' category.

One very simple example is that of membership of a leisure centre. The actual membership could be classed as a tangible product, since the fee gives the member a card showing valid membership. The use of the centre and its facilities, on the other hand, is a service, and customer satisfaction here will depend upon all the usual factors.

activity

Most towns have a cinema either in the town centre or as part of a complex on the outskirts of town, which may have several screens in one building. Most film premieres, on the other hand, are held in London at well-known cinemas, and are usually attended by the press and celebrities and, occasionally, royalty. State the main differences between a local cinema and one in the West End of London. How would the products and services differ?

PRODUCTS AND MARKET SEGMENTS

We said earlier that it is important to get the right product to the right people. How do you know who the right people are?

Very few products will appeal to all the population, and for marketing purposes we divide the population up into sections. The correct terminology is *market segments*, and if you imagine the world as a big orange, representing the 'market', the segments of the orange represent different sections of the market.

In your class you could divide yourself up into several different market segments. Three ways in which you could be divided up for marketing purposes include:

- by gender
- by age
- by race

There are several other recognised categories also. You may wish to divide the market according to:

- geographical location
- social class or grade
- marital status
- lifestyle/occupation

IDENTIFYING CUSTOMER REQUIREMENTS

The reason we need to define these various categories is because different sectors of the market have different needs. We have to identify these needs so that we can keep the different sectors happy.

First, we look at our existing customers, and then at how we compare with other establishments:

1 Customers/consumers — what do they want/expect? How can we find out?
2 Competitors – what are they good at? What could they do better?
3 Us – what are *we* good at? What could we do better? Could we improve our advertising, booking methods, style, facilities, service standards or staffing – or anything else?

THE BROCHURE

It may be that our brochure is boring, or out of date, or maybe doesn't show us in a very good light. Hotel brochures, for example, always show large and spacious rooms, but this is often not because the rooms are actually big, but because of the angle from which the picture is taken.

The brochure is your main sales vehicle – so it must be professional. While everyone wants to show their establishment in the best possible light, remember that you must not lie. The law protects the consumer, and organisations which supply brochures which misrepresent may be prosecuted under the Misrepresentation or Trade Description Act 1968. Remember also that a good-quality

London

EXCLUSIVE HOTELS
BY FORTE

Experience the ultimate in excellence and take a Forte Leisure Break at one of the three luxurious London hotels which feature in the prestigious Exclusive Hotels by Forte collection and you are assured of gracious and discreet service in exquisite surroundings. Individually furnished bedrooms provide every modern comfort and convenience in a traditionally elegant and uncommonly spacious setting. Public rooms are graced with fine furniture, antiques and objets d'art and connoisseurs of fine food and wine will discover the hotels' restaurants are amongst the very best the capital can offer.

Brown's Hotel

Albemarle Street
London W1X 4BP

One of London's most discreet and gracious hotels, Brown's enjoys an excellent location in the heart of Mayfair, near Buckingham Palace, St James' Palace, the Royal Academy and Bond Street. Famed for its afternoon teas, served in one of the traditional, wood panelled reception rooms of this former 19th century townhouse, the hotel offers a high standard of accommodation. Day membership can be arranged for guests to use leisure facilities at the nearby Grosvenor House.

• 110 bedrooms & 6 suites • Brown's Restaurant • Drawing Rooms • St. George's Bar • Open fires in winter • Day membership of leisure facilities at nearby Grosvenor House (£8 per day) • 24 hr room service • Hairdryer, satellite TV • FAMILY: Free baby listening - notice required

Hyde Park Hotel

66 Knightsbridge
London SW1X 7LA

Wonderfully located for Harrods, Harvey Nichols and other legendary Knightsbridge stores, this magnificent marble-halled hotel enjoys a leafy Hyde Park setting and has been one of London's great institutions since 1908. The high standards demanded by the well known resident chef, its elegant yet informal style and individually furnished spacious rooms are just some of the features that ensured the Automobile Association awarded 5 Red Stars in 1994.

- *185 bedrooms including 19 suites & 1 four poster • Restaurant on the Park*
- *'The Restaurant' Marco Pierre White, winner of 3 Michelin Stars*
- *The Bar & Lounge • 24 hr room service • Fitness Centre • Theatre Desk*
- *NCP pay car park nearby • Hairdryer, satellite TV*
- *FAMILY: Babysitting - notice required, & cots on request*
- *SUITE SUPPLEMENT £50pppn*

36

TO BOOK CONTACT YOUR LOCAL TRAVEL AGENT

Figure 2.3 Examples of pages from holiday brochures by Forte and Jarvis Hotels.

Make full use of your FREE Embassy Leisure Breaks Leisure Card

Leisure Breaks Leisure card

LYNDHURST, NEW FOREST
*Lyndhurst Park ****

This Georgian country house hotel stands in 5 acres of grounds, and offers peace & quiet with good food. It is well equipped with modern comforts.

▮ All rooms with private facilities with bath/shower. ▮ Colour TV ▮ Tea & coffee making facilities ▮ No smoking rooms available ▮ Outdoor heated swimming pool ▮ Tennis courts ▮ Sauna ▮ Snooker table ▮ 59 bedrooms ▮ Private parking ▮ A Forestdale hotel

OUT & ABOUT
▮ New Forest ▮ Broadlands ▮ National Motor Museum, Beaulieu ▮ Lyndhurst Park ▮ New Forest Butterfly Museum ▮ Fursey Gardens ▮ Tall Trees Walk.

SUPERSAVER OFFERS *see page 8*
▮ One night in seven FREE

	Mar - Jun 96	Jul - Oct 96	Nov 96 - Apr 97
Dinner Bed & Breakfast	£56.00	£56.00	£56.00
Bed & Breakfast	£42.50	£42.50	£42.50

Hotel Code LYNLYN ⇌ Lyndhurst Road

RINGWOOD
*St Leonards Hotel ****

The hotel is situated in beautiful woodland on the outskirts of the New Forest. Offering a warm and friendly welcome, the newly refurbished pub/restaurant serves excellent cuisine to suit all tastes and appetites.

▮ All rooms with private facilities with bath/shower. ▮ Colour satellite TV ▮ Trouser press ▮ Tea & coffee making facilities ▮ 33 bedrooms ▮ Executive suites available at a supplement ▮ Private parking ▮ A Countryside hotel

OUT & ABOUT
▮ Beaulieu ▮ Corfe Castle ▮ Poole Harbour ▮ New Forest ▮ Swanage ▮ Poole

SUPERSAVER OFFERS *see page 8*
▮ Stay Sunday for just £25
▮ One night in six FREE

	Mar - Apr 96	May - Sep 96	Oct 96 - Apr 97
Dinner Bed & Breakfast (Weekends only)	£45.00	£45.00	£45.00
Bed & Breakfast (Weekends only)	£27.00	£32.50	£32.50

Hotel Code RINSTL ⇌ Bournemouth

STOCKBRIDGE
*The Grosvenor Hotel ****

Prominently located in the High Street of this attractive old market village, the Grosvenor Hotel, formerly a Georgian coaching inn, retains much of its original character. The hotel offers modern facilities including a snooker room and sauna. The Test valley is ideal for fly fishing and most other country pursuits.

▮ All rooms with private facilities with bath/shower ▮ Colour TV ▮ Tea & coffee making facilities ▮ Snooker room ▮ Sauna ▮ 25 bedrooms ▮ Private parking ▮ A Countryside Hotel

OUT & ABOUT
▮ Beaulieu Motor Museum ▮ Stonehenge ▮ Broadlands ▮ Cathedrals of Winchester & Salisbury

SUPERSAVER OFFERS *see page 8*

	Mar - Apr 96	May - Sep 96	Oct 96 - Apr 97
Dinner Bed & Breakfast (Weekends only)	£45.00	£47.50	£45.00
Bed & Breakfast (Weekends only)	£32.50	£33.00	£32.50

Hotel Code STBGRO ⇌ Winchester

BROCKENHURST, NEW FOREST
*Forest Park ****

This attractive country house hotel, set on the outskirts of the picturesque village of Brockenhurst, which offers a warm and friendly welcome all year round. The restaurant offers an excellent menu, including vegetarian specialities.

▮ All rooms with private facilities with bath/shower. ▮ Colour TV ▮ Tea & coffee making facilities ▮ No smoking rooms available ▮ Outdoor heated swimming pool ▮ Riding stables on premises, £14 per hour ▮ Tennis courts ▮ 38 bedrooms ▮ Private parking ▮ A Forestdale hotel

OUT & ABOUT
▮ Bustling village of Brockenhurst ▮ New Forest Museum ▮ Holy Bush Vineyard ▮ Hurst Castle ▮ Bucklers Hard ▮ Beaulieu Motor Museum ▮ Ober Water.

SUPERSAVER OFFERS *see page 8*
▮ One night in seven FREE

	Mar - Jun 96	Jul - Oct 96	Nov 96 - Apr 97
Dinner Bed & Breakfast	£56.00	£56.00	£56.00
Bed & Breakfast	£42.50	£42.50	£42.50

Hotel Code BROFOR ⇌ Brockenhurst

Figure 2.3 continued.

brochure sells, but don't make it so good that it is too expensive to give away! Some organisations include the tariff on a separate piece of paper so that any increase in this tariff can be updated easily without having to renew the whole brochure.

activity

1 Collect some examples of brochures from tour operators, leisure centres and hotels, and compare the content and sales technique.
2 Ask in your IT session if you can produce a brochure to put in your portfolio.

ASSIGNMENT

1 Collect publicity and brochure information from two leisure and tourism facilities in your surrounding area that are competing for the same customers. They should be offering different products and services. Compare the information, and discuss in pairs which facility produces the most eye-catching, user-friendly literature. Is one far more popular than the other? If so, why? How could the other improve its image, product or service to attract more customers?

2 Prepare a short presentation comparing the facilities, giving reasons for their success or failure, and make recommendations for improving customer usage. Besides the provision of products and services, take price into consideration as well.

THE PRICING STRATEGY

When prices can be flexible, they are often adjusted to appeal to, or attract, a wide range of market segments. Everyone is familiar with discounts and special offers, which have become a way of life, but it is important to realise that these also play a vital role in the leisure and tourism industries.

activity

Working in pairs, make a list of actual examples of price adjustments in the leisure and tourism industries.

Your list for the above activity should have included at least some of the following discounted, seasonal and special-offer price rates:

- reduced prices for children
- group rates
- reduction for the day of sale (e.g. theatres)
- reduced prices for late-booked holidays
- off-peak rates for tourist attractions
- off-peak rates for non-peak times in leisure centres
- reductions for series events
- free introductory gifts
- family tickets
- two for the price of one
- weekend breaks
- money-off coupons

Some organisations may also introduce *loss leaders*. Here, one item is priced very cheaply (e.g. a basic burger) while every other item is sold out at the usual price. The idea is that people will initially come in because the burgers are cheap but will then buy fries and a coke to go with it.

Cash rebates are another common way of enticing the market to buy. 'Collect so many labels and send off for one pound back' is a simple example.

activity

Give one example of how each of these pricing strategies could be used in the leisure and tourism industries.

You may find that sometimes business decreases because an organisation offering a similar product or service

Figure 2.4 Examples of special offers from Colchester Zoo and Kew Gardens.

opens up close by. Most people will usually try the new facility at least once.

Sometimes, as a result of pricing restrictions, it is not possible to reduce a price, or there is a price level below which the product or service cannot fall if you still wish to make a profit. If the item is a tangible product, there will have been costs incurred in either producing it or buying it from someone else. Furthermore, you may have spent some money on promoting the product, and this too needs to be covered. And you may also be aware that the market is simply quiet: it may be the period after Christmas and the New Year, for example, or it may be the mid-summer period when many people are away.

In summary, quite a number of other factors contribute to decisions over pricing, such as:

- the season
- unexpected competition
- the economic situation
- legislation

It is up to management to make the correct decision regarding pricing by working out at what stage they will cover costs (i.e. *break even*) and then begin to make a profit.

activity

1 A class has decided to hire a 53-seater coach to visit a local theme park. The cost of the coach is £318.00. How much will each passenger have to pay in order for the venture to break even?

2 On a second occasion, the coach costs £318.00 and the class also needs to give the driver £10.00 for his meals. Four people (who are organisers) will travel free of charge. If each fare-paying passenger pays £7.50

   i what is the break-even point, and

   ii what will the total profit be?

This same simple calculation can be applied to more complicated situations, such as the point at which the price of a package holiday, airline seat or hotel room can be reduced, or the calculation of the number of people needed at a big match before free or reduced tickets can be made available.

activity

You may wish, in your Application of Number class, to work out a *graph* for break-even.

The marketing cycle – see Figure 2.5 – is continuous. We should be constantly looking at what we have, and planning how to maintain our market share or – better still – improve it.

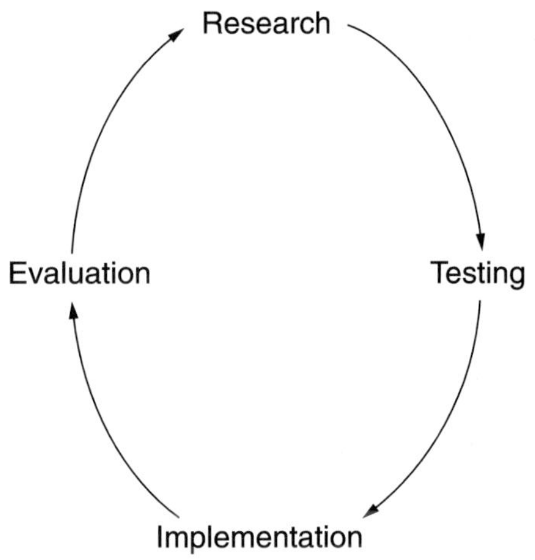

Figure 2.5 The marketing cycle.

Planning a leisure and recreation or travel and tourism promotional campaign

Sales promotions can range from a variety of localised events to a multimedia campaign. The promotion may involve something as simple as informing the public about a change in opening hours: this would involve the staff distributing leaflets and maybe placing an advert in the local papers or perhaps a banner outside. The opening of a totally new facility, however, would need a much higher-profile campaign in order to attract the attention of as many people as possible.

THE OBJECTIVES OF A PROMOTIONAL CAMPAIGN

A campaign may be *informative* – which means it is giving out information. Or it may be *persuasive* – trying to persuade you to buy one product rather than another. Or it could be *educational* – trying to teach you something. Whatever the point or the objective of the campaign, it will almost certainly try to *attract attention* in a variety of ways and to create an *interest* in the product in question. Once this interest has been raised, it is then essential to *hold* it, or even to create a greater degree of interest through a variety of promotional aids.

A successful promotional campaign seeks to improve sales and consequently to increase profits.

PLANNING THE CAMPAIGN

Consider the following example. A hotel, sited on the river Nea, has a very low occupancy rate at weekends. The General Manager has approached a local sailing club to join his campaign, and proposes to offer all-inclusive rates for accommodation, meals and sailing lessons.

Since this would be a totally new venture, an action plan must be drawn up.

activity

For the above venture:

1 define the target market
2 conduct the appropriate market research
3 re-evaluate the target market
4 plan a promotional campaign
5 prepare a promotional campaign
6 implement the promotional campaign
7 evaluate the promotional campaign.

The action plan may carry dates, for when tasks should be performed by, and a space to note down who will be responsible for each task. It is a good idea to have a column for notes.

1 *Define the target market.* Remember that the market is divided into segments, and that we need to decide which of those segments may be interested in our package. Check back to the various segments we have already identified. Will any groups be eliminated? Are some more likely to be interested than others?
2 *Conduct the appropriate market research.* Remember the two types of data: primary and secondary. Which is likely to be more appropriate? How would you carry out research?
3 *Re-evaluate the target market.* Once you have done your research, you *may* find you have targeted the wrong market. Therefore, always keep an open mind, and always check the *results* of your survey.
4 *Plan a promotional campaign.* What are you promoting? To whom? By which media? How much will you spend? What is your target? Can you afford to advertise on radio/TV or in specialist magazines or the national press. If you *do* use any of these media, how will you know if they were worth it?
5 *Prepare a promotional campaign.* Produce product leaflets, book advertising space, train staff, check timing, forecast costs, check legality.
6 *Implement a promotional campaign.* Distribute leaflets, check that adverts appear, ensure that staff are ready, have alternative offers ready.
7 *Evaluate the promotional campaign.* Measure the effectiveness of the campaign. Will it produce or increase business? How will you know? How can you measure? Was it worth it – i.e. did we make a profit? If we didn't make a profit, did we at least break even (remember how to calculate break-even?)? Would we do it again?

Your first draft plan for the hotel package could be laid out as shown in Table 2.1. Dates and tasks could be added at a later date. Clearly, for an event of this type there is no need to employ an advertising agency or to engage a publicity officer.

Table 2.1 Joint package for hotel and sailing club

Objective	To increase occupancy and revenue in the hotel and contribute to profits in the sailing club.
Target market	Either sex: wide age range, approx. 18–65: fairly high disposable income, within reasonable driving distance. Interest in sailing. Previous hotel guests.
Conduct market research	By survey: either through personal interviews, mail surveys or telephone surveys.
Re-evaluate target market	Survey may show (e.g.: of no interest to those with families, or those who already have some sailing knowledge).
Plan promotional campaign	Define product; firm up target market; fix budget; select media: TV – costly; poster – limited audience; local/national newspaper; good specialist magazine; hotel mailing list. Fix target occupancy for break-even.
Prepare promotional campaign	Meet to draft main points to include in publicity: locations, total cost of package, what is included. Draft and produce leaflets, check they are within the law. Ensure staff briefed. Book advertising. Produce brochures.
Implement campaign	Hand out leaflets in reception/club up to three months in advance. Include these with reservation confirmations. Ensure staff use personal selling skills. Check adverts appear. Follow up enquiries. Monitor staff.
Evaluate campaign	Calculate no. of enquiries and no. of actual bookings. Analyse (if possible) reasons why some enquiries didn't book. Compare nos. booked this year with previous years figures. Calculate cost of campaign, including for adverts, postage, printing etc. Deduct share for sailing club. Calculate profit.

activity

1 Give one example of both a leisure event and a tourist activity which would use the services of an advertising agency.

2 Give one example of both a leisure facility and a tourism operation which would employ a publicity officer.

Another way of raising the profile of an event is through sponsorship. This is particularly popular in the leisure sector, where games and matches of all types and at all levels are sponsored by big companies. In tourism also it is becoming increasingly popular, with some major events now seeking sponsorship in order to attempt to offset ever-increasing costs.

There are a range of opportunities associated with promotional campaigns, and it is very important to ensure that planning is done carefully, or the event could be a disaster!

Figure 2.6 Littlewoods are the sponsors of the FA Cup.

Running and evaluating a leisure or tourism promotional campaign

activity

Decide upon an event which you would like to promote. It may be

- a competitive sport against another school or college
- a trip you have organised which you want to promote
- your own course on the school or college Open Day

Using the previous example as guidance, prepare a promotional plan for the event of your choice. Be sure to evaluate its success in terms of both financial gain and knowledge that you gained during the procedure.

In summary:

1 Products are items provided for sale.
2 Services are something provided for clients.
3 Facilities are something used by clients.
4 The factors which affect a client's use of products and facilities are:

- **i** money (disposable income)
- **ii** time
- **iii** location
- **iv** interest/motivation
- **v** ability
- **vi** accessibility
- **vii** a healthy and safe environment
- **viii** security.

5 The market refers to the total number of people who may buy our products or services. It is often divided into various categories, and it is important to remember that different products and services will appeal to different market segments.

UNIT TWO
test YOURSELF

1 The marketing mix comprises place, product, promotion and
- *a* population
- *b* people
- *c* price
- *d* profit.

2 Divisions made by age, gender, race and lifestyle would be classed as divisions into
- *a* market portions
- *b* market segments
- *c* target markets
- *d* market mix.

3 Primary and secondary research is also known as
- *a* product research
- *b* promotional activities
- *c* target markets
- *d* market research.

4 When planning a promotional campaign, the correct sequence of events would be
- *a* planning, implementation, research, preparation and evaluation
- *b* research, implementation, preparation, planning and evaluation
- *c* planning, research, implementation, evaluation and preparation
- *d* research, planning, preparation, implementation and evaluation.

5 If planning a promotional campaign for a small local florist, the most suitable type of medium to use would be
- *a* a local newspaper
- *b* a national newspaper
- *c* television
- *d* a trade magazine.

6 Which of the following is sponsorship as used by a local leisure centre?
- *a* giving money-off coupons
- *b* offering raffle tickets with membership
- *c* offering free swimming lessons
- *d* giving money to a local youth basketball team.

7 A national hotel company wants to raise the public's awareness of its group. Which of the following is a long-term strategic promotion designed to achieve this?
- *a* a draw with a prize of a free stay in a hotel of the group
- *b* a special offer of free children's accommodation
- *c* regular advertising with a theme
- *d* complimentary fruit and flowers in the rooms.

8 A local restaurant offers price reductions for meals which are taken before 8 pm. The main reason for this promotion is to
- *a* encourage usage during quiet periods
- *b* provide extra work for employees
- *c* be able to employ more staff
- *d* allow the chef to order in bulk.

9 Advertising, sales promotion, public relations, personal selling, direct marketing, sponsorship and the product of brochures are all types of
- *a* promotional activity
- *b* market research
- *c* market segments
- *d* media.

10 The success of a promotional campaign could be measured by
- *a* the amount spent on postage
- *b* an increase in sales
- *c* a decrease in customers
- *d* higher costs in the warehouse.

11 Advertisements, leaflets, brochures, posters and notices are all types of
- *a* evaluations
- *b* promotional material
- *c* marketing
- *d* promotional campaigns.

12 Which of the following should be carried out in order to decide if a promotional campaign has been successful?
- *a* a discussion
- *b* participation
- *c* a recommendation
- *d* an evaluation.

13 If a theme park is running a campaign to promote its latest rides, the success of the promotional campaign will be best evaluated by the number of
- *a* visitors on the latest rides
- *b* booking enquiries
- *c* souvenirs sold in the shop
- *d* visitors to the park.

14 A local visitor attraction is designing a promotional campaign to attract families with young children. The most suitable feature to emphasise in the campaign would be
- *a* guided tours lasting two hours
- *b* play and activity areas
- *c* wheelchair access
- *d* opening times.

15 Bad publicity has been seen in local newspapers regarding a local attraction. In order to rectify this, the attraction should
- *a* do nothing and hope that not many people read the reports
- *b* send a mailshot to local residents
- *c* advertise the positive reports from recent visitors
- *d* offer discounted entrance fees.

16 Why might a pub decide to invest in a 'children's room'?
- *a* it will shortly be a legal requirement
- *b* staff may bring their children to work
- *c* more customers will be encouraged to come
- *d* people are less likely to get drunk.

17 It is common for a new hotel to invite travel agents to its opening. The main reason for this is
- *a* they will give an honest opinion
- *b* hotel staff will get discount holidays
- *c* the hotel will not have a sufficient number of customers at first
- *d* travel agents will be able to see the facilities and sell them.

18 The most common market segments are divided according to
- *a* age
- *b* street
- *c* education
- *d* nationality.

19 The most likely choice of medium to advertise an exhibition in a museum is
- *a* television
- *b* radio
- *c* direct mail
- *d* a newspaper.

20 Which of the following activities is classed as promotional?
- *a* team-building
- *b* sponsorship
- *c* staff parties
- *d* renovation.

21 A theme park does a mail drop which includes a free ride after entry. The main reason for this is to
- *a* promote new rides
- *b* encourage families to return
- *c* analyse new trends
- *d* encourage new business.

22 Competition between similar establishments is most likely to be resolved by
- *a* increased advertising
- *b* reducing prices
- *c* increasing the number of services on offer
- *d* providing quality services.

23 'Two for the price of one' is *most* likely to be on offer
- *a* in a hotel
- *b* from a tour operator
- *c* in a public house
- *d* by a travel agent.

24 An increase in sports activity in a local centre is *most* likely to have been caused by
- *a* government health reports
- *b* discount vouchers
- *c* cold winters
- *d* promotional campaigns.

25 Explain what is meant by primary and secondary market research.

26 Explain why market research is essential when planning a promotional campaign.

27 List the type of media which may be used when planning a promotional campaign for an international company.

28 Name the four basic and interlinking parts which make up the marketing mix.

29 Give examples of at least six different price structures which may operate in a sports/leisure centre.

30 Give examples of how the success of a promotional campaign may be measured in
- *a* a cinema
- *b* a travel agent
- *c* a theme park
- *d* a golf course.

31 What is the difference between field research and desk research?

32 List six different market segments in the leisure and tourism industries.

33 Explain why a leisure centre may target one market segment for particular slots.

34 Briefly state the effect that inaccurate or inappropriate research data may have on a promotional campaign.

CASE STUDY

A car-hire company has recently taken over a smaller competitor in the same town. The competitor had a range of vehicles in their fleet, including luxury limousines and two minibuses. Since the merger, which took place four months ago, neither of the minibuses have been rented out, and only one of the limousines has been hired – and only once at that. (The rest of the fleet has been absorbed into the main stock and is causing no real concern.) The area manager has noticed that there is a potential problem here, and has asked you to look into it and make a report with appropriate recommendations. When you study the records which came with the fleet, it becomes clear that they have not been rented out for some time. Some research by you turns up the name of the company that last rented the minibus, and you call them to see if they will be using the service again. The reply is short and not very polite: apparently the bus was filthy when they picked it up, and it broke down on the M1. What's more, the cover which was included with the rental had not been paid, so the breakdown service would not come out. A similar story was told by the people who last hired a limousine.

A week after your meeting with the area manager, you attend a conference held by the local tourist board, and are seated next to a hotel owner who has only one property located in the forest close to the golf course. You discover that the hotel is facing serious competition from larger hotels and chains that can afford to advertise and to retain courtesy cars and buses to fetch clients from the station and the airport. Staying on after the conference, you outline some ideas to the hotel manager relating to joint promotions and advertising. Clearly, there is some scope here, since both organisations may benefit from a deal.

1. Design a brochure which could be used as a mail drop to advertise this partnership.
2. Construct an advertisement to be placed in the local newspaper.
3. Research the costs involved in placing the advert in two different local newspapers. Explain *why* the two costs might be different.
4. Summarise the main advantages and disadvantages of joining forces.
5. Produce a report, to be given verbally or written, about future ideas for increasing the rental of the minibus and limousines.

unit 3

Customer service in leisure and tourism

At the end of this unit, you should have:

- I learned about the importance of effective customer service to the leisure and tourism industries
- II learned about the importance of information in providing customer service
- III recognised that sales and selling are an integral part of customer service
- IV delivered customer service in three relevant situations, and then evaluated your own performances.

Explaining the principles of customer service in leisure and tourism

Customer service, and all that it entails, underpins our entire industry (and for that reason you will find it overlaps with many other topics). We care about our customers because we want them to come back: if they enjoy their experience of our product or service, they will want to repeat it. They may also tell their friends. This is free advertising for us, and the best sort we can have.

Customer service is a part of every job in every sector of the leisure and tourism industries.

activity

Which of the illustrations below represents good customer service?

In the above activity, you may have selected the top illustration. This is fine, but if the services shown in the bottom two illustrations were poor, the customer may never have reached the situation shown in the top illustration.

WHAT IS CUSTOMER CARE?

Customer care is more than just being nice to your customers: you must also learn to judge your customer's mood, and to control your own. Any industry which deals with people will have problems – people are the most unaccountable factor in any industry. There will be times when you do not feel like helping or assisting others – particularly if they are proving difficult – but this is what you have chosen to do, and if you intend to do it well you must always present a positive attitude. Your interpersonal and communication skills are your best asset. Customer needs are many, and varied. Customers may be asking you for help or information, or for advice if they are unsure of something. The way in which you answer their enquiry will give them an impression about the level of service in the establishment. If you answer well, the customer will be satisfied, and will almost certainly return (thereby increasing profits). If you answer badly on a regular basis, the consequences for both you and the facility could be very bad. The way in which you communicate is therefore very important.

Customer service involves the entire experience of dealing with customers, and is not only concerned with just the face-to-face interaction with the customer – though, this face-to-face part of the service is often the easiest. The customers are with you for a reason. They want something, for example:

- a holiday
- some information
- a game of squash

In other words, they have *needs* which you should be able to meet. They may want help or advice about your product or service, and if you want success for yourself and your company you must be in a position to provide this service. Remember, service does not necessarily mean being servile, but rather being cheerful and helpful regardless of how people treat you. Even if your customers are presenting a negative attitude, you will feel better about yourself and your job if you remain polite, positive and enthusiastic. Often, you will find that your positive attitude rubs off on others so that colleagues will feel better, and that customers may compliment you for a job well done. Regardless of other outcomes, you will feel better about yourself knowing that you are performing your job to the best of your ability. All types of tourism and leisure work are a form of service, and if you can relate your service to a challenge, which can be a lot of fun, your positive attitude will always show through.

Figure 3.1 Positive and negative attitudes

Quite evidently (as Figure 3.1 illustrates), customer service is a vital part of our image. We have already realised that it may be the reason why the client comes back, and *repeat* business is vital, so we aim to give *customer satisfaction*, which in turn will encourage *customer loyalty*. If, then, the customer brings friends, or just *tells* friends – or, even better, a company – we will benefit from both increased sales and increased profits. And remember it is not only the customer and the company that benefits: *you* will enjoy increased job satisfaction.

SOCIAL SKILLS IN CUSTOMER CARE

Social skills have been defined in many different ways, but at the very least they include politeness, good personal presentation, a positive attitude (with a smile), and a pleasant disposition or personality. To define exactly what is meant by social skills, we could say that it is the ability to adapt your behaviour so as to fit in with different everyday scenes. For example, few students would behave in the same way with a group of their lecturers as they would with a group of their fellow students (or their peer group). Most of us gain experience early in life about the different roles we will have to play, and we learn to adapt our behaviour accordingly.

activity

Make a list of all the different roles you play, starting with that of:

- student

In the above activity, did you include any of the following roles?

- son or daughter
- sister or brother – maybe both younger and older?
- grandchild
- boyfriend or girlfriend
- shop assistant (or whatever your Saturday job involves)

For most people, a list like this is only the beginning – you will certainly be able to think of several other roles.

Those who display good social skills will find themselves equally at home in any situation. This is not to say that they have a 'split personality' or that they are two-faced, but simply that they are able to adopt a different style in keeping with different situations.

Social skills can therefore be summarised as follows:

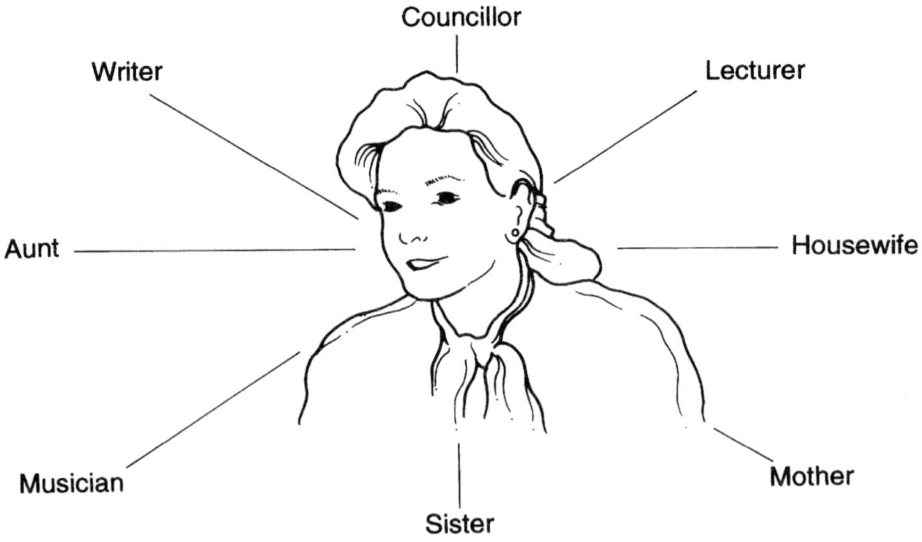

Figure 3.2 The roles one might play in life.

i politeness
ii good personal presentation
iii a positive attitude
iv a pleasant disposition.

> ***activity***
>
> A swimming pool is closed for repairs and decoration. Say how you would inform each of the following customers when they arrive, using your social skills:
>
> **1** two 10-year-old children
> **2** a mother and toddler
> **3** lunch-time swimmers
> **4** a retired couple.

In the above activity, did you think of the following points?

1 The 10-year-old children are not really interested in why it is closed: they would just need to know when it will be open again and what else they could do instead.
2 The mother would want to know why it was closed – was it a safety problem? – and when it will be open again.
3 Give a reopening date, and suggest the nearest alternative pool or other alternative activities.
4 Had they come specially? Were they out of pocket? Maybe offer a free swim when the pool reopens.

This is a good example of direct customer service. If you know the pool is closed, you make yourself available to explain this to customers, and try to make sure they are not disappointed. An example of *indirect* customer care would have been to display notices, in advance, warning of the forthcoming closure, or to write to regular users. Good indirect customer service can also often result in a more satisfied customer, and produce more positive results for the facility.

In tourism and leisure, we are dealing with every type of customer in the world:

- old–young
- poor–rich

> ***activity***
>
> Think of at least two other pairs of opposites which you are bound to encounter.

In the above activity, did you think of 'polite–rude', 'experienced–beginners'? Because we are dealing with so many people, we need to possess a wide variety of skills, particularly in *communication*. Customer care is about communicating with people, and giving the right signals. Communication can be of two types: *verbal* and *non-verbal*, and understanding and using these correctly is an essential feature of customer care.

VERBAL COMMUNICATION SKILLS

Verbal communication is not about speaking Queen's English but about speaking *clearly*, so that the client can understand you. It is also about *listening*, which is an important part of communication. And it is also important to remember that we do not speak to customers as we would speak to our friends: with the former, we need to show politeness – i.e. 'Please', 'Thank you', 'May I help you?' – in our verbal communication.

NON-VERBAL COMMUNICATION SKILLS

Non-verbal communication, or *body language*, is the way in which we can communicate with each other without the use of words.

> ***activity***
>
> Make a list of all the non-verbal communication skills found in everyday use.

In the above activity, you probably thought of:

- smiles
- nods
- gestures
- eye contact
- gazing

Did you also think of:

- posture or stance
- facial expressions
- head movements
- proximity?

A smile or a nod can convey a welcome, or indicate to a client that you have seen them even though you may be on the phone or dealing with another customer. A gesture can indicate a waiting area where visitors may sit, or that you will be a few moments before you can deal with their needs.

Eye contact is very important. It shows attention and interest, and provides feedback during conversations: it tells you if you are recognised, liked, disliked and a wealth of other information. Remember that on most occasions a direct and open gaze is preferable to an avoidance of eye contact, which is usually interpreted as insincerity or shiftiness (only very experienced liars will meet your eye).

A correct posture is important for all sorts of reasons. If you sit or stand badly you will make yourself feel tired, and you may experience back problems later in life. Your posture can also portray an image: it may be welcoming or forbidding, relaxed or threatening, and many other things.

The expressiveness of the face is second only to that of the eyes. Facial expression shows our emotional state and our attitude to others – we can show surprise, fear, pleasure and many other things without uttering a word.

A head movement can signify agreement, disagreement, enquiry or the emphasising of an important point. But be careful: in some parts of the world a shake of the head means agreement!

Proximity is another important factor in communication. Everyone has their 'space' around them, and if someone you do not know invades your space you feel uncomfortable. This 'invasion' often produces nervousness and restlessness, and people will adopt a protective pose.

INTERNAL AND EXTERNAL COMMUNICATION

As well as non-verbal and verbal communication skills, we also need to be aware of the differences between *internal* communication with our colleagues and *external* communication with our customers.

1 Internal communication involves:

i *verbal* communication:

- face to face
- interviews
- meetings
- customer reception
- public address systems
- paging
- telephones
- sign language
- walkie-talkies

ii *printed* communication:

- computer networks
- photocopies
- memos
- posters
- internal circulars
- transparencies
- notices

2 External communication involves:

i *verbal* communication:

- telephones
- CB radios

ii *printed* communication:

- letters
- telexes
- faxes
- magazines
- newspapers, local and national
- trade journals
- circulars, mailshots
- electronic mail
- telephone directories
- guides
- government publications
- computer networks

When choosing the method of communication best suited to the purpose, the following must also be taken into account:

i speed – to what extent is this a prime factor?

ii a record – is this essential (as proof of communication)?
iii accuracy – you may be misinterpreted over the telephone and misunderstood
iv safety – do you need a record of receipt (recorded or registered mail)?
v confidentiality – is this necessary?
vi cost – how important?

Investigating the provision of information as part of customer service

Everyone can recall some experience when the person serving them could not answer what seemed to be a simple question. While no-one can be expected to know everything, all employees, as well as learning good communication and interpersonal skills, must know certain basic information relating to their job:

i the products for sale
ii the cost and availability of the products
iii opening and closing times
iv security procedures
v the organisational structure.

The exact information you will be expected to know will of course vary with the job, and it ranges from the whereabouts of the nearest toilet to knowing whether or not the Queen is in residence. The information you would need to know in a tourist information centre would be vast. At the minimum, this might include:

- brochures
- maps
- local events
- local and specialist papers
- YHA information
- sporting events

Work through the next activity. In number 2, did you include guide books, refreshment information, a local map or map of the grounds where appropriate, and opening and closing times?

The key to the effective provision of information is to ensure that you have considered what customers are likely to want to know. Much of this may come with experience, but until then, put yourself in the customer's place and ask yourself 'What would my needs be?' If a customer asks you a question and you don't know the answer, say so, but offer to find out – and make sure you *do*, because someone else may ask you the same question tomorrow.

Many of our customers are from overseas, particularly in the tourism sector, and this is where the above-mentioned non-verbal communication skills become important when providing information as part of customer services, since verbal communication may be limited. Speak clearly (don't shout) and use signs to illustrate your meaning. If the customer still can't understand you, trying writing it down: it is often easier to recognise a word when it is written rather than spoken.

activity

1 As a group, compile a complete list of information needed in a busy tourist information centre.
2 What about the information needed in a stately home or a museum?

activity

Draw a map which will direct a visitor to the canteen/refectory in your building. Add direction signs if it will make the route clearer.

ASSIGNMENT

1 Telephone two hotels: one country hotel and one city hotel. Request a brochure and a tariff, and enquire if they offer any special rates for weekends. Also, ask for information about Christmas and New Year packages.

From your observations, comment upon the time spent waiting for the hotels both to answer the

IMPORTANT •GUEST• INFORMATION

Welcome to Granada Studios Tour.

By planning ahead, you'll be able to see the various shows on site either before or after your Backstage Tour. This leaflet, together with the showtime boards*, should contain everything you need to plan your day - but if you require further help, just ask at the Information Booth situated in the middle of New York Street.

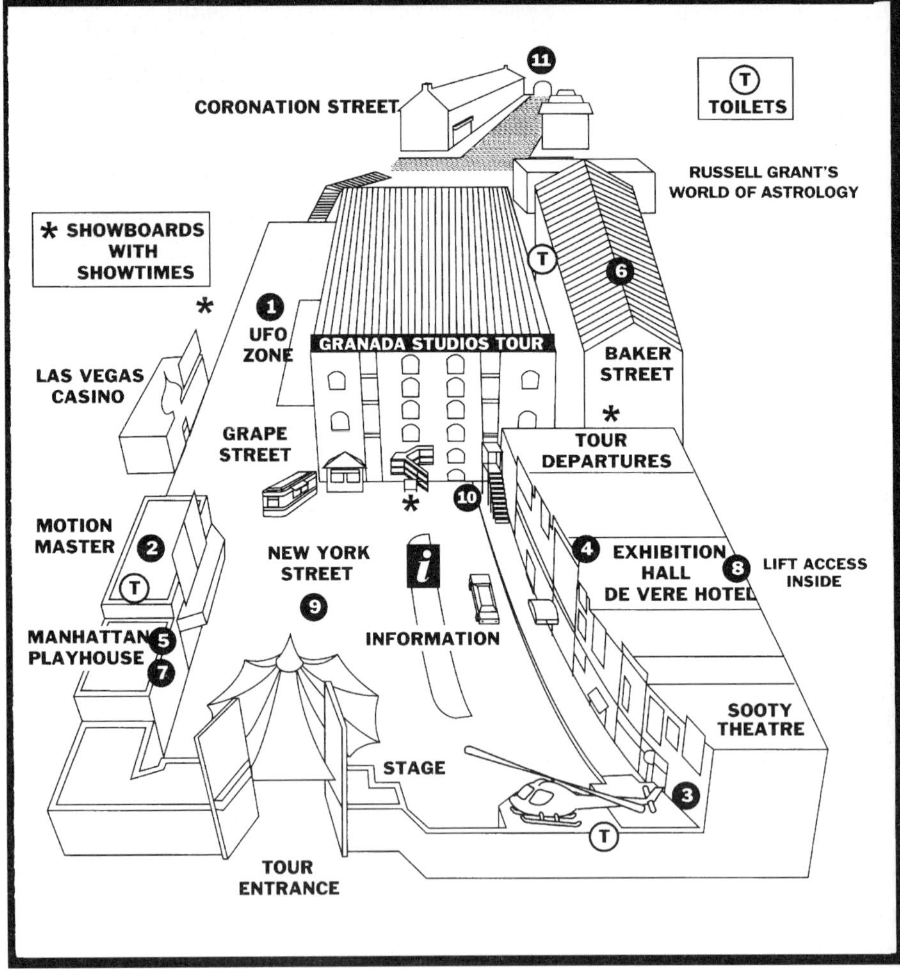

1
UFO ZONE

★ ★ ★

2
MOTIONMASTER

★ ★ ★

3
THE SOOTY SHOW

★ ★ ★

4
HOUSE OF COMMONS SHOW

★ ★ ★

5
DEADLY F/X

★ ★ ★

6
BAKER STREET SET

★ ★ ★

7
SOUNDS SPECTACULAR

★ ★ ★

8
3-D SHOW

★ ★ ★

9
NEW YORK STREET

★ ★ ★

10
BACKSTAGE TOUR/ TOUR DEPARTURES

★ ★ ★

11
CORONATION STREET

Figure 3.3 Examples of customer information supplied by Granada Studios and Kew Gardens.

GRANADA · STUDIOS · TOUR

IMPORTANT ·GUEST· INFORMATION

1 U.F.O. ZONE

An alien spaceship has crash-landed!
Dare you investigate this area?
Be warned! -
Not all life forms have been accounted for.
This ride includes lighting and smoke effects and may be unsuitable for certain guests.
Not for the faint-hearted!
Throughout the day.
Buy your souvenir photo from the UFO shop.

2 MOTIONMASTER

ROBO-COP
Fasten your seatbelts as we fast forward to the 21st Century and MotionMaster - the cinema of the future, where the seats move with the action.
Certain restrictions apply.
Not suitable for disabled guests.
20 minutes.
Opposite New York Street.
Throughout the day.
Wurlitzer Organ playing throughout the day.

3 THE SOOTY SHOW

Britain's best loved teddy bear in a show especially created for youngsters.
On New York Street.
25 minutes.
Minimum 10 children required.
Please see showboard for times.
Sooty souvenirs available from The Sooty Shop next door.

4 HOUSE OF COMMONS SHOW

Join the hilarious comedy debate.
Your chance to lay down the law.
30 minutes.
Through the De Vere Hotel.
On New York Street.
Please see showboard for times.
Lift access in De Vere Hotel.

5 DEADLY F/X

THE SPECIAL EFFECTS SHOW
This show reveals some of the more horrific tricks of the trade, as our two experts battle it out.
PG Some scenes may not be suitable for children or those of a nervous disposition.
30 Minutes.
This show alternates with the Sound Effects Show.
Please see showboard for times.

6 BAKER STREET SET

Don't miss this unique undercover set.
Visit 221B & see if the great Detective is at home or enjoy some musical entertainment with the Baker Street Players · Music Hall, Singalongs or Street Theatre.
Open all day. Access via New York Street Staircase.
Please see showboard for times.

7 SOUNDS SPECTACULAR

THE SOUND EFFECTS SHOW
Add sound effects to the film or watch the hilarious attempts of others. It's not as easy as it looks!
30 minutes.
This show alternates with the Special Effects Show.
Opposite New York Street.
Please see showboard for times.

8 3-D SHOW

A choice of two shows:
Haunts of the Olde Country
The Rock Laser Show
Put on your special glasses and dive for cover as stunning visual effects leap out of the screen.
20 minutes.
(Smoke machines and lasers used during performance.)
Through the De Vere Hotel.
On New York Street.
Please see showboard for times.
Lift access in De Vere Hotel.

9 NEW YORK STREET SET

Explore the sights and sounds of downtown New York. Have your picture taken with our Tour Mascots and visit our shops and restaurants.
Watch out for the Cop strolling his beat.
Musical entertainment throughout the day.
Information Booth situated in the centre of the street 'Let us Help You Plan Your Day'.

10 THE BACKSTAGE TOUR

Enjoy a fascinating guided tour behind the scenes of TV and film making.
See some of Coronation Street's famous interior sets.
Your tour has a fixed time OR a designated number. Listen out for your tour being announced.
Entrance at Tour Departures, New York Street.
60 minutes.

11 CORONATION STREET

Your chance to walk down the most famous cobbled street in the world.
Visit the Coronation Street Experience and relive some magical moments from the show's history.
Visit the Street before or after your Backstage Tour.
Enter via Baker Street.
RESTRICTIONS MAY APPLY DUE TO FILMING.
Coronation Street souvenirs available from Rosamund Street shop and our Coronation Street shop on Grape Street.

1 UFO ZONE
★ ★ ★
2 MOTIONMASTER
★ ★ ★
3 THE SOOTY SHOW
★ ★ ★
4 HOUSE OF COMMONS SHOW
★ ★ ★
5 DEADLY F/X
★ ★ ★
6 BAKER STREET SET
★ ★ ★
7 SOUNDS SPECTACULAR
★ ★ ★
8 3-D SHOW
★ ★ ★
9 NEW YORK STREET
★ ★ ★
10 BACKSTAGE TOUR/ TOUR DEPARTURES
★ ★ ★
11 CORONATION STREET

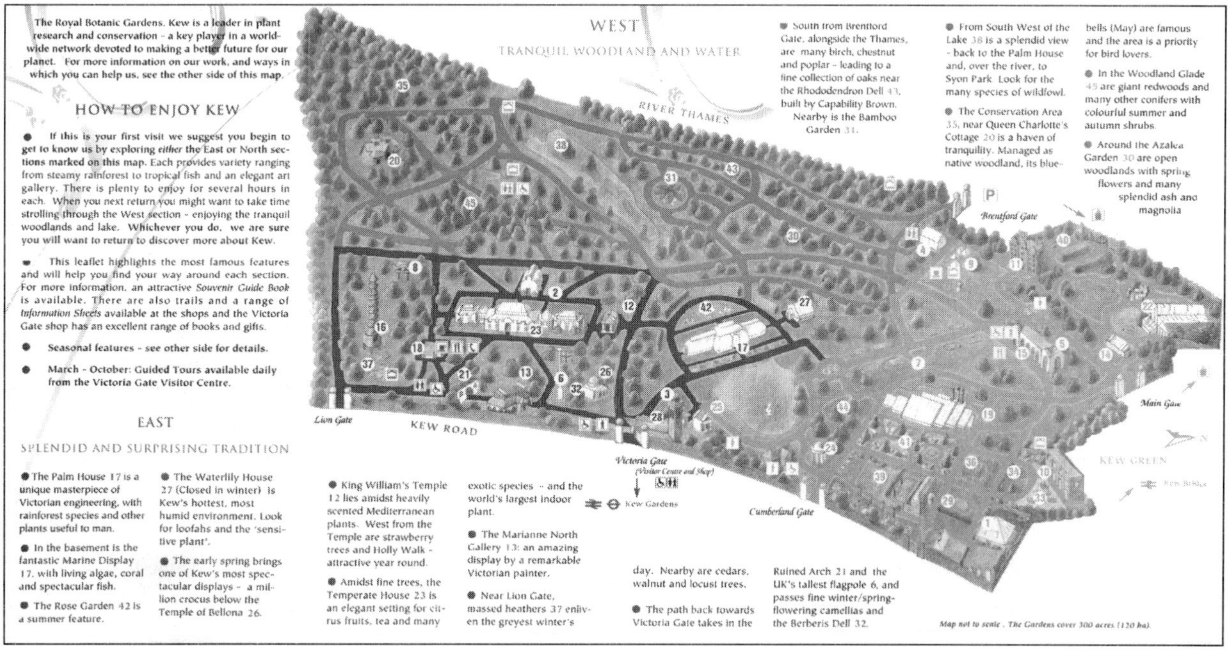

The Royal Botanic Gardens, Kew is a leader in plant research and conservation – a key player in a world-wide network devoted to making a better future for our planet. For more information on our work, and ways in which you can help us, see the other side of this map.

HOW TO ENJOY KEW

- **If this is your first visit we suggest you begin to get to know us by exploring *either* the East or North sections marked on this map.** Each provides variety ranging from steamy rainforest to tropical fish and an elegant art gallery. There is plenty to enjoy for several hours in each. When you next return you might want to take time strolling through the West section - enjoying the tranquil woodlands and lake. **Whichever you do, we are sure you will want to return to discover more about Kew.**
- This leaflet highlights the most famous features and will help you find your way around each section. For more information, an attractive *Souvenir Guide Book* is available. There are also trails and a range of *Information Sheets* available at the shops and the Victoria Gate shop has an excellent range of books and gifts.
- **Seasonal features - see other side for details.**
- **March - October: Guided Tours available daily from the Victoria Gate Visitor Centre.**

EAST

SPLENDID AND SURPRISING TRADITION

- The Palm House 17 is a unique masterpiece of Victorian engineering, with rainforest species and other plants useful to man.
- In the basement is the fantastic Marine Display 17, with living algae, coral and spectacular fish.
- The Rose Garden 42 is a summer feature.
- The Waterlily House 27 (Closed in winter) is Kew's hottest, most humid environment. Look for loofahs and the 'sensitive plant'.
- The early spring brings one of Kew's most spectacular displays – a million crocus below the Temple of Bellona 26.
- King William's Temple 12 lies amidst heavily scented Mediterranean plants. West from the Temple are strawberry trees and Holly Walk - attractive year round.
- Amidst fine trees, the Temperate House 23 is an elegant setting for citrus fruits, tea and many exotic species – and the world's largest indoor plant.
- The Marianne North Gallery 13: an amazing display by a remarkable Victorian painter.
- Near Lion Gate, massed heathers 37 enliven the greyest winter's day. Nearby are cedars, walnut and locust trees.
- The path back towards Victoria Gate takes in the Ruined Arch 21 and the UK's tallest flagpole 6, and passes fine winter/spring-flowering camellias and the Berberis Dell 32.

WEST

TRANQUIL WOODLAND AND WATER

- South from Brentford Gate, alongside the Thames, are many birch, chestnut and poplar – leading to a fine collection of oaks near the Rhododendron Dell 43, built by Capability Brown. Nearby is the Bamboo Garden 31.
- From South West of the Lake 38 is a splendid view - back to the Palm House and, over the river, to Syon Park. Look for the many species of wildfowl.
- The Conservation Area 35, near Queen Charlotte's Cottage 20 is a haven of tranquility. Managed as native woodland, its blue-bells (May) are famous and the area is a priority for bird lovers.
- In the Woodland Glade 45 are giant redwoods and many other conifers with colourful summer and autumn shrubs.
- Around the Azalea Garden 30 are open woodlands with spring flowers and many splendid ash and magnolia

Figure 3.3 continued.

telephone and to give you the required information. How helpful were they? What was the overall impression you had of the hotels? Would you want to book accommodation there?

2 Draft a letter to send to two hotels: one country/resort hotel and one city hotel. Request information as a prospective guest on any special weekend packages (bargain weekends) available in the New Year. How long did you have to wait before the information arrived? Was there a personalised letter? was the information useful and clear, and would it have made you book accommodation?

Investigating and demonstrating sales techniques as part of customer service

It cannot be stressed often enough that good customer services is one of the best sales aids you will ever have – it costs nothing in outlay, except perhaps some staff-training costs. Those of you who have Saturday jobs will be familiar with the 'Will there be anything else?' approach (for example, a bag to match the shoes). There are many ways of providing customers with a good service while at the same time increasing sales. Why do you think they give away crisps and peanuts in bars? Well, it keeps the customers happy, yes, but it also makes them thirsty so they buy *more* drinks. The combination of good customer service and good salesmanship is not hard, but it is essential for survival.

Holiday reps depend upon selling excursions for their commission, but if they are to be successful the customers must feel as if the excursion is there for *their* benefit or else they will not buy. Retail outlets in leisure and tourism organisations do indeed look as if they are there for the convenience of the customer, yet they also pay a commission to the establishment, which all contributes to profits. The wide range of memberships available in most clubs seems to cover all aspects and combinations – single people, partners, families etc. Convenient for the customer? Yes, but convenient for us too: a special offer may increase membership, which in turn increases profits.

All sales contribute to the profit, and if the customer feels *satisfied* as well, that is an added bonus. Sales techniques are linked closely to customer service, for they are both dependent on the same skills. A good sales person must be able to create a good first impression which will then give the customer confidence. This can be done in a variety of ways, but a smart personal appearance and pleasant open manner are both very positive attributes which will help. A well-known hotel company had a big poster, which it displayed in staff areas, which read 'You never get a second chance to make a good first impression.'

Professional sales people will always try to sell up (remember the shoes and the bag mentioned earlier?), but this must be done in such a way that the customer does not feel pressurised. Sales on a face-to-face basis are easiest, because you can make use of non-verbal skills and information: i.e. you can judge your customer's reactions. If you quote a price and see a flicker of alarm on their faces, then you can offer something cheaper – other selling methods do not have this advantage. Various studies have shown that non-verbal signals are five times more revealing of a person's true feelings or disposition than are verbal comments. There is much truth in the expression that it is not what is said but *how* it is said.

Consider the following two approaches:

1 'Membership fees are going up again.'
2 'You'll be glad to know we found the towel you left last week – I've put a list of the new membership prices with it – and I'm pleased to say we have been able to reserve your usual court.'

Now the second approach is of course much longer, and it takes more time, but it *softens the blow about the increases*. The Americans call this 'sandwich selling': the filling is the bad news, which they then try to cover on both sides with something *positive*.

Another way of providing a customer service and of scoring positive sales points is in the use of the customer's name. This shows you have an interest in the customer, and it makes them feel important. You should use the customer's name during conversation whenever you can – rather than 'Sir' or 'Madam', which is so impersonal.

Telephone sales are the next best method of selling, because even here you can still get a general impression of the customer's response. It is not as clear as in a face-to-face conversation, since you are missing all the visual clues, but a slight hesitation, some doubt or reluctance in the tone, should tell you all is not well. It may be the price, the venue, the date, all manner of things, and it is up to you to find out what the problem is.

Consider the following two approaches:

1 'So I could offer you that resort either the week before or the week after. What do you think?'
2 'That resort has a vacancy the week before you wanted it, or the week after. Can you get away earlier?'

The first leaves the choice to the customer – it is an open question. The customer may reply by saying 'I'll think about it', in which case you have lost your opportunity. The second is a closed question: the response is really yes or no, and it is forcing the customer to decide. If the customer says no, an earlier break is impossible. You can then switch to the later option. Again the response is still yes or no. If the answer is no, the ball is back in your court, and you are still free to make some other suggestions.

Regardless of how hard we try, sometimes there will be complaints. Some are justified, others are not, but if we are to keep the customer happy they must all be dealt with. Here are a few simple rules:

1 Try to move the customer away from the public area – particularly if they are complaining noisily.
2 Take down the main points of the complaint.
3 Assure the customer that you will bring it to the attention of the appropriate person, and that you will advise the customer of the outcome. Then, make sure that you *do both those things*.
4 Always refer serious complaints directly to management.
5 Do not defend yourself, your colleagues, the facility, the service or anything else.

Whatever the complaint is about, the customer will feel better for having verbalised it – and even if you are not the right person, you can help by listening intelligently.

Providing and evaluating customer service in leisure and tourism

Many organisations now have a customer care policy which guides their staff in the handling of clients. This is usually prominently displayed, and used as a reminder to staff for when they are dealing with customers.

activity

1 List some well-known organisations that have recently published customer care policies.
2 Do you have a part-time evening job? Can you bring your employer's customer care policy in to share and discuss with your group?
3 How do you think management make the decision about what to include in a customer care policy?

Before a policy can be decided upon, customers' needs and expectations need to be analysed and then discussed with management and employees. A series of relevant questionnaires could be circulated to staff to find out both how they perceive the customer and whether they feel any improvements could be made in the way they handle them.

Customer questionnaires sent to, say, existing members at a leisure/sports complex or a travel agency customer along with their tickets enable customers to highlight their likes and dislikes. Guest questionnaires placed in hotel bedrooms to encourage a response have also become very common, and most major companies now encourage communication in this way. Where the clientele is international, the questionnaire may even be printed in more than one language (see P&O example).

A questionnaire really serves two purposes: it allows a customer to say exactly what they think of a place, but it also enables them to do so without having to complain in public. Although some clients do enjoy the latter activity, many are quiet or retiring and would never complain openly; instead, they would simply not come back – or even worse, they would talk about it to their friends.

Britannia

It is of the utmost importance to Britannia that our passengers have an enjoyable and comfortable flight. I would be pleased to receive your comments and suggestions about any aspects of our service, such as check-in facilities, inflight meals, drinks, duty free sales, inflight video and the attentiveness of cabin staff. We regret that we cannot give individual replies, but rest assured that your comments will receive our careful attention.

____

FOLD 1

FOLD 2

Your Name ________________________________

FLIGHT DETAILS

1. UK Airport ____________________
2. Overseas Airport ____________________
3. Flight Nos ____________________
4. Date of Flight ____________________
5. Tour Operator ____________________
6. Aircraft Type 757/767-200/767-300
7. Seat Number ____________________
8. Outward/Homeward Journey (delete where applicable)

Roger Burnell Managing Director

Please seal the envelope and hand it to our cabin staff or post it on your return to the UK. Thank you for your help

Figure 3.4 Examples of customer questionnaires supplied by Britannia and Thomson.

Thomson Incorporating

HORIZON Skytours PORTLAND

CUSTOMER SATISFACTION SURVEY

Enjoyed your holiday? We hope you have, because we work very hard to ensure that our customers have a really good time. But we need your help to make things even better. Your opinions are very important to us, and by completing this questionnaire you will help improve the standard and quality of future holidays.

All questionnaires are returned to RSL, an independent market research company. The answers to the questions are analysed and the results take the form of regular reports on levels of customer satisfaction. Please take the time to complete the questionnaire, regardless of whether you are a first time holidaymaker, or a regular customer. Thank you.

Please ☑ appropriate box, or write in answer as requested

YOUR HOLIDAY DETAILS...

▶ **Which holiday company are you with?**

Thomson [1] Skytours [3]
Horizon [2] Portland [4]
Other [5] ➡ Write in .... (21)

▶ **Was this holiday:**

Full board [1] Self catering [4]
Half board [2] Room only [5]
Bed/breakfast [3] Flights only [6] (27)

▶ **The name of your resort(s) or the name of your tour/safari/cruise**

....

....

▶ **The name of your Hotel(s)/Villa/Apartments (name all accommodation stayed in)**

....

....

▶ **Number of nights abroad:**

6 or less [1] 14 [4]
7 [2] 15-20 [5]
8-13 [3] 21 or more [6] (23)

▶ **Was the name of your accommodation specified:**

In advance [1] On arrival at resort [2] (25)

If in resort, was this a:

Late availability/Square Deal [1]
Price Breaker [2] (26)

▶ **How did you book this holiday?**

Direct with holiday company [1]
With a travel agent [2] (102)

▶ **With which travel agent did you book this holiday?**

A.T. Mays [1] Co-op Travelcare [5]
Thomas Cook [2] Callers Pegasus [6]
Lunn Poly [3] Dawson & Sanderson [7]
Going Places [4] Other [8]
Write in .... (35)

▶ **Was this a Young at Heart or Home & Away holiday?** Yes [1] No [2] (24)

▶ **How long before departure was the holiday booked?**

Less than 1 week [1] 5-6 months [5]
1-4 weeks [2] 7-8 months [6]
1-2 months [3] 9-10 months [7]
3-4 months [4] Longer ago [8] (22)

▶ **Not counting this one, how many holidays abroad have you been on in the past three years:**

	None	One	Two	Three or more	
With Thomson/ Skytours/Horizon	0	1	2	3	(86)
With Portland	0	1	2	3	(103)
With other package holiday companies ...	0	1	2	3	(87)
Independently arranged (non-package)	0	1	2	3	(88)
To this resort/island	0	1	2	3	(33)
To this accommodation	0	1	2	3	(32)
Self-catering	0	1	2	3	(34)

Figure 3.4 continued.

FLIGHTS . . .

Please rate:	Excellent	Good	Fair	Poor	
▷ UK airport check-in arrangements	1	2	3	4	(36)
▷ Resort airport check-in arrangements	1	2	3	4	(37)
▷ In-flight comfort	1	2	3	4	(38)
▷ In-flight food	1	2	3	4	(39)
▷ Cabin crew: attitude and manner	1	2	3	4	(40)
▷ In-flight audio/visual entertainment	1	2	3	4	(41)

IN-RESORT SERVICE . . .

	Excellent	Good	Fair	Poor	
▷ On arrival: assistance at resort airport/transfer journey	1	2	3	4	(42)
▷ On departure: assistance at resort airport/transfer journey	1	2	3	4	(43)
▷ Representatives: availability and punctuality	1	2	3	4	(44)
▷ Representatives: attitude and manner	1	2	3	4	(45)
▷ Representatives: knowledge	1	2	3	4	(46)
▷ Welcome Get-Together	1	2	3	4	(47)
▷ Excursions: choice	1	2	3	4	(48)
▷ Excursions: value for money	1	2	3	4	(49)

YOUR ACCOMMODATION . . .

Please give an average rating of all accommodation stayed in.	Excellent	Good	Fair	Poor	
▷ Location	1	2	3	4	(50)
▷ Reception service	1	2	3	4	(51)
▷ Bar service	1	2	3	4	(52)
▷ Cleanliness and maintenance	1	2	3	4	(53)
▷ Comfort of public areas	1	2	3	4	(54)
▷ Bedroom comfort	1	2	3	4	(55)
▷ Breakfast	1	2	3	4	(57)
▷ Midday/evening meals	1	2	3	4	(58)
▷ Waiter service/buffet efficiency	1	2	3	4	(56)
▷ Daytime activities and leisure facilities	1	2	3	4	(60)
▷ Evening entertainment	1	2	3	4	(61)
▷ Villa/apartment equipment	1	2	3	4	(59)

OVERALL . . .

Taking everything into account:	Excellent	Good	Fair	Poor	
▷ Flights	1	2	3	4	(62)
▷ Resort	1	2	3	4	(64)
▷ Accommodation	1	2	3	4	(65)
▷ Representatives	1	2	3	4	(66)
▷ Holiday overall	1	2	3	4	(69)
▷ Holiday company overall	1	2	3	4	(67)
▷ Value for money	1	2	3	4	(68)
▷ Accuracy of accommodation description in brochure	1	2	3	4	(163)
▷ Accuracy of accommodation photographs in brochure	1	2	3	4	(164)

Figure 3.4 continued.

OUT & ABOUT...

▶ **Please rate:**

	Excellent	Good	Fair	Poor	
▷ Holiday weather	1	2	3	4	(63)

▶ **Did you yourself:**

	Yes	No	
▷ Go to the Welcome Get-Together	1	2	(74)
▷ Go on any Thomson company excursions	1	2	(75)
▷ Rent a car for/during your holiday	1	2	(77)

	Excellent	Good	Fair	Poor	
▷ Arrangements for collecting car	1	2	3	4	(78)
▷ Car hire overall	1	2	3	4	(79)

▶ **Booked with:** Hertz [1] Dollar [2] Other company [3] (81)

▶ **Was the car:** Pre-booked in the UK [1] Booked in resort via our Representative [2] Booked independently in resort [3] (80)

ANY PROBLEMS?...

▶ **Did you experience any problems during your holiday?** Yes [1] No [2] (165)

▶ **If yes, what was the nature of the problem?**

Accommodation related [1] Transfers/ Airport arrangements [2] Medical/personal [3]

General advice/information [4] Flight related [5] Other (please specify) [6] (166-171)

(eg. directions/car hire/excursions/currency etc.)

▶ **Regarding this problem, did you contact:**

	Yes	How many times?		No	
▷ A Thomson Representative	1	➡ { Write numbers in boxes } ➡		2	(208)
▷ A member of the cabin crew	1			2	(211)

▶ **How soon after first contact was your problem resolved or otherwise concluded?**

Immediately [1] Within 1 day [2] Within 2-3 days [3]

Within 4-7 days [4] After 8 days or more [5] Never [6] (172)

▶ **Did they resolve your problem?**

Completely [1] Mostly [2] Partly [3] Not at all [4] (173)

▶ **How satisfied were you with the action taken?**

Completely [1] Mostly [2] Partly [3] Not at all [4] (174)

HOLIDAY EXPERIENCE...

▶ **How likely are you to choose a Thomson company for your next package holiday?**

(ie. Thomson, Horizon, Skytours or Portland) Definitely [1] Probably [2] Possibly [3] Not likely [4] (63)

▶ **With which company did you take your last package holiday abroad?**

Thomson, Horizon or Skytours [1] Portland [2] Airtours [3] Cosmos [4] Enterprise/ Falcon [5] (84-85)

Aspro [6] Inspirations [7] Kuoni [8] Sunmed [9]

Sunworld [10] Virgin [11] First Choice [12] Other [13] ➡Write in ....

▶ **Not counting this one, which of the following types of holiday abroad have you taken in the past three years?**

(not necessarily with Thomson companies, all holidays both package and independent)

Cities/short breaks [1] Winter sun holiday [4] Winter sports [7]

Specialist holiday for over 55s [2] Longhaul [5] Lakes & mountains [8]

Summer sun holiday [3] Flights only [6] None [9] (89-96)

Figure 3.4 continued.

ABOUT YOU...

▶ **I am:** Male [1] Female [2] (97)

Married [1] (incl. living with partner) Single [2] (incl. widowed, separated, divorced) (98)

▶ **Age:** 16-24 [1] 35-44 [3] 55-64 [5]
25-34 [2] 45-54 [4] 65 + [6] (99)

▶ **I am:** In full/part time employment or self employed [1] (100)
A student [3] A full time housewife [2]
Retired [4] Otherwise not employed [5]

▶ **If you are in employment, which best describes the type of job you do, or if retired, the last job you did?**

Skilled trade/craft [1] (101)
Plant and machine operator/driver etc. [2]
Foreman/supervisor [3]
Manual worker/factory worker [4]
Service worker (eg. shop assistant/cleaner/catering/caretaker/goods delivery etc.) [5]
Clerical/secretarial/other office work [6]
Technical (eg. programmer/technician/nurse/representative) [7]
Junior management/junior professions/executive [8]
Senior & middle management/professions [9]
Other (write in) .... [0]

▶ **Have you been ill at any time during your holiday?**
Yes [1] No [2] (117)

If yes, please write in illness: ....

▶ **Name:** Mr / Mrs / Miss / Ms Initials
Surname

Address (Street – Town/City)

County

Postcode

Date 199

Please can we assure you that your name and address will not be passed to any third party. However, from time to time we may wish to send you brochures or other details of our holidays. If you would prefer not to receive this information, please tick this box. [1] (109)

▶ **I am travelling (tick all that apply):**

Alone .... [1]
With my husband/wife/partner .... [2]
With infants aged 0-1 .... [3]
With children aged 2-11 .... [4]
With children aged 12-15 .... [5]
With other adult(s) of the same sex ..... [6]
With other adult(s) of different sexes .... [7]
With an organised group of 10 or more... [8]
(175-182)

▶ **Please rate:**

	Excellent	Good	Fair	Poor	
▷ Children's facilities for 2-15 year olds ...	1	2	3	4	(183)
▷ Children's Representatives....	1	2	3	4	(70)

▶ **Which daily newspaper do you read regularly/often?**

The Sun	1	The Express	7
The Mirror	2	Daily Star	8
The Times	3	The Independent	9
The Guardian	4	Today	10
Financial Times	5	Daily Mail	11
The Telegraph	6	Daily Record	12

(184-207)

THANK YOU VERY MUCH! ANY OTHER COMMENTS?

We find your comments interesting and helpful, but are unable to reply to individual questionnaires. If you have a problem and would like a specific reply please write separately to: Thomson, Customer Service, Greater London House, Hampstead Road, London NW1 7SD, or Portland, Customer Service, 218 Great Portland Street, London W1N 5HG.

s95/v1/j5700

Figure 3.4 continued.

Peninsular House,
Wharf Road,
Portsmouth,
PO2 8TA
Tel: (0705) 772000

P&O European Ferries
A MEMBER OF THE P&O GROUP

Quai de Southampton
7600 Le Havre
Tel: (35) 21 36 50

PASSENGER QUESTIONNAIRE

Dear Passenger

Thank you for choosing to travel with P&O European Ferries. We hope that you have a pleasant crossing and that you will find the shipboard facilities to your liking.

Our aim is to provide you with the highest possible standards of service. In order to help us plan future facilities, we would be pleased if you would answer this questionnaire.

If you are not completely satisfied with any aspect of your crossing, please do not hesitate to see the Chief Purser.

We look forward to welcoming you on board our vessels again in the future.

YOUR CROSSING

Ship ______ *Date* ______ *Time* ______

From ______ *To* ______ *Cabin No.* ______

Name ______

Address ______

______

______ *Telephone No.* ______

PROFESSION ______

SERVICE

Are you happy with the standard of service you have experienced? ☐ Yes ☐ No

Have our staff been friendly and efficient? ☐ Yes ☐ No

Comments ______

CABINS

Was your cabin clean and properly prepared? ☐ Yes ☐ No

Comments ______

REFRESHMENTS

Did you find the range, quality and presentation of our food was to the standard you expected? ☐ Yes ☐ No

Comments ______

SHOPS

Did you find the range of goods for sale met with your expectations? ☐ Yes ☐ No

Are there any additional items you would like to see on sale? ______

______

OTHER COMMENTS

______

______

Please hand this card to the Hostess in the Information Office, or send it to the Customer Relations Executive at our Portsmouth address.

Figure 3.5 Examples of customer questionnaires using more than one European language, supplied by P&O and the Aeneas Hotel in Cyprus.

Peninsular House,
Wharf Road,
Portsmouth,
PO2 8TA
Tel: (0705) 772000

P&O
European Ferries
A MEMBER OF THE P&O GROUP

Quai de Southampton
7600 Le Havre
Tel: (35) 21 36 50

QUESTIONNAIRE A REMPLIR PAR LE PASSAGER

Cher passager

Nous vous remercions d'avoir voyagé avec P&O European Ferries. Nous espérons que vous avez effectué une traversée agréable et que les services à bord vous ont donné entière satisfaction.

Notre but est de vous fournir un service de haut niveau. Pour nous permettre d'améliorer notre qualité de service, nous vous serions reconnaissants de bien vouloir répondre à ce questionnaire.

Si vous n'êtes pas entièrement satisfait des prestations à bord, n'hésitez surtout pas à contacter le 'Chief Purser'.

Nous espérons vous accueillir de nouveau à bord très bientôt.

VOTRE TRAVERSEE

Navire ______ *Date* ______ *Heure* ______

De ______ *à* ______ *Cabine No.* ______

Nom ______

Adresse ______

______

______ *Tél* ______

PROFESSION ______

SERVICE

Etes-vous satisfait de la qualité du service dont vous avez bénéficié? ☐ *Oui* ☐ *Non*

Notre personnel a-t-il été courtois et efficace? ☐ *Oui* ☐ *Non*

Commentaires ______

CABINES

Votre cabine était-elle propre et bien préparée? ☐ *Oui* ☐ *Non*

Commentaires ______

RESTAURATION

La sélection, la qualité et la présentation de nos produits répondaient-elles à votre attente? ☐ *Oui* ☐ *Non*

Commentaires ______

BOUTIQUE

La sélection des articles en vente vous a-t-elle donnée satisfaction? ☐ *Oui* ☐ *Non*

Y a-t-il d'autres articles que vous souhaiteriez voir en vente? ______

______

AUTRES COMMENTAIRES

______

______

______

Veuillez remettre ce questionnaire à l'hôtesse au bureau d'information à bord ou envoyez-le à notre bureau de Portsmouth à l'attention du 'Customer Relations Executive'.

Figure 3.5 continued.

DEAR GUEST,

We should like to know how well we have met your needs and expectations during your stay. Your comments will help us to ensure the standards you expect and deserve.

Please leave this card at the reception and your comments will come to my personal attention.)

Thank you for having chosen to stay with us. We look forward to welcoming you again soon.

Sincerely yours,

Andreas Antoniou
General Manager

VEREHRTER GAST,

Lassen Sie uns bitte wissen, ob wir Ihre Wünsche und Erwartungen während Ihres Aufenthaltes erfüllen konnten. Ihre Meinung wird uns helfen, Ihnen einen gleichbleibend hohen Standard zu gewährleisten.

Bitte hinterlegen Sie diese Karte an der Rezeption.

Wir bedanken uns für Ihren Besuch und würden uns freuen, Sie bald wieder in einem unserer Hotels begrüßen zu dürfen.

Mit bester Empfehlung,

Andreas Antoniou
General Manager

Why did you select our hotel?
Weshalb haben Sie unser Hotel gewählt?

What did you like most about it?
Was hat Ihnen bei uns am besten gefallen?

What could be improved?
Was Könnte (Ihrer Meinung nach) verbessert werden?

Please let us know who of our staff were the most helpful, so that we can show them our appreciation:
Bitte lassen Sie uns wissen, welcher Mitarbeiter sich als besonders hilfreich erwiesen hat.

NAME:

ROOM NUMBER:
ZIMMER-NR.

DATE:
DATUM:

ADDRESS:
ADRESSE:

COMMENTS & SUGGESTIONS
KOMMENTARE & EMPFEHLUNGEN

Figure 3.5 continued.

activity

For each of the following situations, list ways in which customer care could be employed, *plus* any financial costs which could be incurred.

1 A guest wants to move to another, similar room but with a better view.
2 A client complains about changing-room facilities left dirty because the cleaner is off sick.
3 A group complain to their courier that the continental breakfast which is included in the tour rate is inadequate.
4 Regular customers to a leisure centre are dissatisfied at being unable to get games at peak times (e.g. bank holidays).

Customer care is important for all clients in leisure and tourism, but most especially for those with special needs.

activity

Go around your building and identify positive and negative points of customer care in relation to disabled people.

MAINTAINING RECORDS

Many establishments keep records of their regular clients. This ensures that we know their likes and dislikes, and it also means we can measure how frequently they use our facility. Records can be kept manually or on a computer, but however they are kept they will contain some information which is personal to the client, so it is essential that they are kept securely.

UNIT THREE *test* YOURSELF

1 Customer services means
- *a* a wide range of goods and services are on offer
- *b* customers will be well cared for
- *c* customers will get 24-hour service
- *d* the staff will all be very servile.

2 A gardener in a stately home will
- *a* have direct customer contact
- *b* have indirect customer contact
- *c* not be part of the customer care programme
- *d* have a leading role in the customer care programme.

3 The main reason why staff should provide good customer service is
- *a* management may be watching
- *b* customers may leave tips
- *c* management may pay a bonus for good customer care
- *d* customers will be satisfied and may return.

4 Which of the following combinations of i–vi shown in a–d is most likely to contribute to customer satisfaction?
- *i* looking smart
- *ii* offering help
- *iii* smiling
- *iv* product knowledge
- *v* a safe environment
- *vi* new uniforms.

- *a* i, iii, v
- *b* i, ii, iii
- *c* ii, iv, v
- *d* iii, iv, vi.

5 A facility which offers good customer service is *most* likely to
- *a* charge more than its competitors
- *b* charge less than its competitors
- *c* experience a high staff turnover
- *d* experience more repeat business.

6 The best way to reply to a customer who has written raising some points relating to customer service is
- *a* wait until they visit next time and apologise
- *b* reply by fax
- *c* write a letter explaining how customer service will be improved
- *d* telephone the customer.

7 Who would a tour operator involve when reviewing a customer care programme?
- *a* the travel agent
- *b* a representative
- *c* the receptionist
- *d* airline staff.

8 Customer loyalty is most likely to be achieved by
- *a* offering discounts
- *b* sales promotions
- *c* a good service
- *d* new facilities.

9 Which of the following provides the *best* opportunity for good customer service?
- *a* contact by letters
- *b* face-to-face contact
- *c* use of non-verbal skills
- *d* communication by fax.

10 The *main* reason a tour operator would want to provide effective customer service is that
- *a* customers may not return if dissatisfied
- *b* they may lose their licence if someone complains
- *c* hotels will not do business with them if the guests are complaining
- *d* customers may tell other people if they are dissatisfied.

11 The best way of communicating with a non-English-speaking customer is
- *a* speak loudly and clearly
- *b* face the customer and speak clearly
- *c* write everything down
- *d* use signs and gestures.

12 Which of the following combinations of i–iv shown in a–d is most likely to be used to satisfy customer needs when on holiday?
- *i* newspapers
- *ii* brochures
- *iii* trade journals
- *iv* maps
- *v* accommodation listings
- *vi* national association publications.

- *a* i, ii, iii
- *b* ii, iv, vi
- *c* ii, iii, iv
- *d* iii, v, vi.

13 Which of the following are essential when providing good customer service?
- *a* a detailed knowledge of products
- *b* a knowledge of prices
- *c* IT skills
- *d* a college qualification.

14 Which of the following customer services are passengers touring by coach most likely to require at stops?
- *a* a wide variety of gift shops
- *b* good toilet facilities
- *c* a comprehensive menu
- *d* a public telephone.

15 A client at a leisure-centre reception is asking for details of family membership, but reception is very busy. The best way to help is
- *a* ask the client to come back later
- *b* suggest they telephone during the week
- *c* offer written details to read until the rush is over
- *d* ask for the name and address, and offer to send information.

16 The type of customer service which would be most suitable in a museum is
- *a* friendly and brisk
- *b* slow and methodical
- *c* polite and friendly
- *d* polite and knowledgeable.

17 The main reason for trying to create a positive first impression is so that customers will

- ***a*** spend more money
- ***b*** feel more relaxed
- ***c*** engage staff in conversation
- ***d*** spend more time on their activity.

18 The *main* reason a holiday representative will sell excursions is that

- ***a*** the hotel gets commission
- ***b*** the local tourist board expects it
- ***c*** it will add to the customers' enjoyment
- ***d*** it will increase the customers' knowledge.

19 Which of the following of i–vi shown in a–d is most likely to result in customer sales?

- ***i*** smiles
- ***ii*** gestures
- ***iii*** frowns
- ***iv*** a positive attitude
- ***v*** a good posture
- ***vi*** an open stance.

- ***a*** i, ii, iii
- ***b*** i, iv, vi
- ***c*** ii, iv, v
- ***d*** iii, v, vi.

20 The *main* reason for keeping a list of customer names and addresses is that it

- ***a*** is a legal requirement
- ***b*** is required for tax purposes
- ***c*** can be sold as a mailing list
- ***d*** can be used to promote future business.

21 The *main* reason that leisure-centre staff are trained in health and safety is that

- ***a*** work will be done more quickly
- ***b*** work will be done more economically
- ***c*** customers will be safer and more secure
- ***d*** customers will be more likely to spend money.

22 A beauty-salon reception keeps confidential records of all the salon's clients and their treatments. The best system would be

- ***a*** near at hand in reception
- ***b*** alphabetically in a box file
- ***c*** limited access on computer
- ***d*** open access on computer.

23 A large group of overseas visitors is checking into a UK hotel. The quickest and easiest method of registering them is to

- ***a*** set up a special desk to deal with this group
- ***b*** go on the coach and give out the keys
- ***c*** ask the courier to hand out the keys
- ***d*** check them in as ordinary guests.

24 Which of the following services in a hotel room is most likely to be appreciated by a customer who is deaf?

- ***a*** a large TV screen
- ***b*** bedside volume controls
- ***c*** a selection of audio tapes
- ***d*** an induction loop.

25 Which of the following facilities are most likely to maintain records of visitors?

- ***a*** a museum
- ***b*** a theme park
- ***c*** a cinema
- ***d*** a leisure centre.

26 List four reasons why customers will return to a facility.

27 Give four ways in which staff can make a customer's stay enjoyable.

28 List four benefits to organisations which should be achieved by good customer care.

29 Briefly explain why customer feedback is an important part of a customer care policy.

30 Explain the major problems which will be found when trying to deal with customer complaints by telephone.

31 List eight publications which would normally be available in a library.

32 Using your classroom as a base, give clear directions to a partner to the nearest exit assuming that your partner speaks limited English.

33 Explain why different age groups and different cultures have different holiday and leisure needs.

34 The following is an extract from a sales conversation: 'I'm pleased you decided to call in rather than phone. Tell me something about your organisation.' 'Would you like coffee? Fine, we'll go and see the facility.'

a Which of the above is an open question?
b Which of the above is a closed question?

35 Refer to the conversation above and state how the sales situation could have been followed through if the customer had failed to turn up for the appointment.

CASE STUDY

A holiday village on the south coast of England comprises a number of chalets of varying sizes, a central block with a restaurant, bar and games room, and outdoor activities such as tennis, a children's play area and pool. The majority of customers arrive by car, or the complex provides a courtesy minibus from the station if requested, at no extra charge. Most people arrive on Saturday, although a few also arrive on Friday or Sunday. Weekday arrivals are quite rare, and most of the staff are given their time off during the week, when the complex is not busy with arrivals and departures.

At about 12.30 pm one Friday in July, when most of the customers are either in the bar or already in the restaurant, a party arrives: two young women and five children, several suitcases, beach-balls, sun umbrellas and a small surfboard. One of the women is extremely angry, complaining loudly and shouting at the children, one of whom begins to cry. There is no one in reception at this time, as they receive few enquiries while everyone is at lunch and so take the opportunity to have their own break. Several of the customers come out of the bar to see what the fuss is all about, and the bar manager sends a member of staff to find someone from reception.

When the receptionist arrives, the lady who has been complaining gives vent to her feelings, which centre mainly upon the fact that: they were promised a courtesy coach, which didn't arrive; no one answered the phone when they rang; and they couldn't find a taxi, and when they did it wouldn't take all of them. By the time they had found a second cab, the first had already got £5.20 on the meter, and the whole journey, which was interrupted because one of the children was sick, cost them £25.90. The receptionist tries to calm down the two ladies, both of whom are angry, and asks them to take a seat while the booking is checked. The children go outside to investigate, while the adults try to organise the luggage and look a little less conspicuous.

An investigation by reception shows that the reason the coach did not arrive was that no record of the booking was made, and unfortunately, when the bookings expected all arrive on Saturday, there will be no vacancies. As the receptionist reluctantly starts to explain the situation, one of the women begins an hysterical outburst about where will they go and how will her husband find them because he is away on business in Germany. Several people come out of the bar again to see what is happening, and at this point the oldest child rushes in shouting for help. The 5-year-old was in the children's play area by the pool (which should be locked when unattended) and fell from the top of the climbing frame, landing very badly. He is not moving, and appears to be unconscious.

1. Outline the action which should be taken immediately.
2. Discuss the ways in which the customer-care aspects of this scene could have been improved.
3. Make recommendations about how you will solve the problems concerning this booking.
4. Make recommendations as to how long-term customer care should be improved in this facility.
5. Write a concise report for the management in order for them to give the relevant information to head office.

unit 4

Contributing to the running of an event

> *At the end of this unit, you should have:*
>
> I learned the theory and practice of planning an event with other team members
> II undertaken a role in the event planned
> III carried out an evaluation of the team event.

Planning an event with others

Why organise an event?

- for financial gain: to make a profit
- for the local community
- for promotional/publicity purposes
- for educational purposes

to name but a few reasons.

The first stage in organising an event is to *plan*:

i What are the objectives of the event?
ii What are the options either offered or suggested?
iii What resources are needed in terms of time, people, skills, equipment?
iv Are there any constraints in terms of season, transport, opening times, staff availability?
v Is there any anticipated disruption due to the weather or a change in group numbers?
vi Is the event viable in terms of time, money, resources and people?

The various phases in planning, whether or not they are recorded, must obviously occur in an appropriate order: it would, for example, be silly to first send out invitations to a party if the location had not yet been booked and confirmed. Let us first look at the planning of a birthday party for a school child, Simon. The plan may look something like this:

i Check the availability of the village hall.
ii Book, confirm and send the deposit for the village hall.
iii Entertainer availability and cost: book, confirm and send the deposit if required.
iv Arrange invitations – written or printed – showing the date, time, place and reason, and asking for replies.
v Order a birthday cake.
vi Provisionally book caterers.
vii Prepare the decorations required – streamers, balloons, etc.
viii When replies have been received: finalise the amount and type of food and drink.
ix Prizes for games – buy and wrap them.
x Buy party bags and their contents.
xi Arrange tableware, plates, cups etc. (if themed party).
xii On the day, transport everything to the hall.

Of course, the list on its own is by no means sufficient as there is no mention of the time-scale involved: for example, would the hall or the food have to be booked two weeks, two months or two years in advance? Certain events would have to be booked earlier than others depending upon the popularity of the venue, and it is true to say that a large wedding party may be booked anything up to three years in advance of the occasion.

activity

To ensure the smooth planning of the above children's party, research the relevant details involved (i.e. the costs and time-scales for the different staff and facilities listed above) and enter these onto the action plan in Table 4.1 (the event here is Simon's birthday party, and the date is 19 April). Discuss this plan in class with other students and your lecturer, especially if the time-scales involved vary a lot.

The planning of Simon's party would most likely have been done by one person, either his mum, his dad or his guardian. More people would be involved for a large wedding, a coach outing which would need to be publicised, or an event to be held on behalf of an organisation. Any large event will need to be carefully planned, with people being allocated roles or tasks. This would all be done formally in a meeting.

Undertaking a role in the team event

In order for you as a team member, to hold a meeting, you should be aware of the terms used when holding a meeting. If you are going to hold a properly structured meeting in which everything is recorded and acted upon, you should appoint certain members of the class team to defined roles:

i chairperson
ii secretary
iii treasurer
iv publicity officer

You may also like to refer to the glossary offering explanations used in the running of a successful meeting.

Table 4.1 An action plan

Event:			Date:		
Enquiry date	Person making enq.	Enq. made to	Cost/booked	Confirmation/deposit	Further action

GLOSSARY

Adjourn to hold a meeting over until a later date

Agenda a list of items drawn up for discussion at a meeting

Annual General Meeting (AGM) all members are usually eligible to attend

Apologies excuses given in advance for inability to attend a meeting

Chairperson the person who is given authority to conduct a meeting and is expected to keep order

Committee a group of people usually elected or appointed who meet to conduct agreed business and report back to the main group or a senior body

Consensus agreement by general consent, no formal vote being taken

Convene to call a meeting

Lobbying a practice of seeking member's support before a meeting

Minutes the written record of a meeting; usually circulated to members and then agreed upon

Motion the name given to a 'proposal' when it is being discussed at a meeting

Mover one who speaks on behalf of a motion

Opposer one who speaks against a motion

Order, point of the drawing of attention to a breach of rules or procedures

Other business items either left over from a previous meeting, or discussed after the main business of a meeting

Proposal the name given to a submitted item for discussion before a meeting takes place

Proxy meaning on behalf of another person – a vote made on someone else's behalf

Resolution the name given to a 'motion' which has been passed or carried; used after the decision has been reached

Secretary committee official responsible for the internal and external administration of a committee, and the person who will record the minutes at a meeting

Secret ballot a system of voting in secret

Seconder one who supports the 'proposer' of a motion or proposal by 'seconding' it

Treasurer committee official responsible for its financial records and transactions, and one who gives the financial report to the committee members

Unanimous all being in favour

activity

Using the information provided above, you should now be in a position to plan your own event. By this we do not mean afternoon tea for four people: rather, it must involve either some or *all* of your class team in the planning stages, and it may be for any event for up to 150 people who will hopefully benefit or enjoy themselves – or both. Talk to your lecturer: how large is your team? Is it possible to plan two or three events and then carry them all out – or at least choose the most suitable one – or would you prefer to plan only *one* event in which everyone can be actively involved? If only one event is chosen, will there be a role for everyone? It is very important not to leave anyone out.

You should hold a meeting to hear suggestions from all members as to what type of events to consider. These may include:

- an end-of-year party either in or out of school or college
- a day trip to a local attraction
- a day trip abroad

- a day visit to the theatre
- a weekend visit to a UK destination
- a visit to an overseas resort

At the first meeting, a vote may be taken to establish two or three ideas, and then the members would need to obtain further details before the next meeting:

i dates
ii costs
iii numbers
iv transport
v refreshments
vi accommodation
vii availability

At the second meeting, the members should give a presentation to the committee, and a written proposal should be circulated to all members. There should also be an opportunity for questions to be asked. Then, a final vote should be taken to decide on which event the group will run.

Once an event has been chosen, prepare an action plan which would be relevant to this type of project. One idea might be to use an action plan which looks something like the example in Table 4.1. Each member can have a copy of the action plan, which should be updated at each meeting, and in this way everyone can clearly see the progress made by each member. If someone is not contributing to the planning, this will be made abundantly clear. It is possible that some of the roles may have to be changed if people cannot fulfil them for any reason. In order for the event to be successful, the committee must be flexible enough to allow its members to identify their strengths and weaknesses.

Once the number of events has been decided upon, the members of the committee have been chosen and the initial action plan has been drawn up, each individual member should keep:

i copies of agendas
ii a copy of the minutes for each meeting
iii a copy of the current group action plan
iv an individual action plan
v an individual diary/log sheet.

These should all be kept with your portfolio and used as evidence. If you have been allocated specific tasks and are not able to carry these out for one reason or another, make sure you consult with someone else who may be able to help you so that other members do not feel that you are letting them down. No one minds changes that have to be made so long as they are aware of them, and they know that you have acted in a responsible manner. If a member of your class team cannot help with your particular problem, ask either your present tutor or maybe your key skills tutor for help. Keep a record of events so that you can report back at the next meeting.

At least one of the committee meetings should be recorded on video, and if possible, one video at the beginning, one during the planning phase and one at the final meeting would be preferable. Such a sequence of recordings would show how individuals developed, how the event itself progressed and hopefully the result when all the parts were organised and the members were more relaxed again. It should also highlight those students who were always well-organised, those who adapted quickly to any changes made, and those who perhaps came through at the end with more practical help at the final event.

Your records must always be kept up to date, especially if someone else asks for your help, assistance or ideas on another part of the project, as this can also be used as evidence of teamwork when the evaluation after the event takes place.

When planning your event, it is important to remember that the more ambitious you are the more you have to plan ahead. If you have a big event in mind, you will need to think about certain legal requirements: do you need permission from the police? Should you alert the fire services? And at the very least, should you make some provision for fire outbreaks? Remember, too, that our climate is notorious. If you are planning an outdoor event, is there somewhere to go if it pours with rain all day? Even the most dedicated supporter becomes a little less keen when they are soaked.

Evaluating the team event

This is something which takes place after the event to establish whether it was a success. The following points need to be addressed:

i Did the event meet the original objectives?
ii Did the participants enjoy themselves?

iii Was a profit made?
iv If so, was it what was expected?
v Was anything overlooked?
vi Were all the resources used, and if so, were they used efficiently?
vii What obstacles occurred, and were they overcome?
viii Did everyone who was involved contribute?

activity

As a committee, draw up an evaluation form to be circulated to the people who participated in the event to enable them to comment upon its success or otherwise. You should include the following (but no doubt you can also add other relevant items):

i the name of the event
ii the date
iii how you found out about the event
iv whether or not you considered it to be value for money.

It is advisable to give everyone an *evaluation form* (see the above activity) whilst at the event, and for someone to collect them in at the end. Left to themselves, people will not return them unless they have a major complaint, and this may be an isolated case unrepresentative of the view of the majority of people. It is therefore a good idea to have an incentive for people to return completed forms: for example, they could be numbered, with the owner of the winning number earning a small prize. The information on the collected forms should then be collated, and statistics should be calculated on, for example:

i the number of people participating in the event
ii the number of people returning the evaluation form
iii the specific information given on the form, expressed as a percentage – for example, '20 per cent did not enjoy the event because the weather was bad and they got wet,' or '80 per cent enjoyed the event and the weather did not spoil their enjoyment.'

These figures could be shown on a graph or chart for presentation at the next committee meeting.

If anyone has a serious complaint which is justified, make sure someone writes a letter of apology, even if you are not in a position to offer compensation or a refund: the customer will at least be pleased that you were aware of the complaint and that you will ensure that it does not occur again.

A *team evaluation form* should be drawn up next, and should include sections for:

i attendance rates
ii profits
iii individual performance
iv team performance
v recommendations
vi the overall level of success.

Each member should complete an evaluation form, and all these forms should be made available at the final meeting for discussion. There will be a number of questions that will probably be asked at the final meeting, and these may include:

i Did we enjoy the challenge?
ii Did everyone contribute on an equal basis?
iii Does any particular member need special thanks for a specific task?
iv Did we learn something from this event?
v *Would we do it again?*

activity

If your class undertook the planning and running of more than one event, once the evaluation meeting has taken place you should:

i write a report, or give a presentation, and include a copy of an evaluation form
ii mention any of the event's strengths or weaknesses, plus any recommendations for improvements should another event similar to the first one be taking place.

One member of your group should make a presentation to the rest of the class and allow time for questions and discussions.

Sometimes you will find that what, at a given time, was expected to be particularly important/stressful for a member of your group passed very smoothly and without incident, whereas something which you may have thought very insignificant ended up causing major problems on the day. Can any improvements be suggested for a similar future event?

At an evaluation meeting, it is possible for some hostility to take place between members, and whilst no one likes to give credit to someone who did very little, it is also very unprofessional to blame one person in front of everyone else. Instead, a mention could be made to indicate that something was amiss, and suggestions made for improvement in future, without embarrassing anyone by name. Also, an opportunity should be given (if required) for that particular person to explain why their task was problematical: it may have been through no fault of their own, and they may have already made constructive suggestions for improvements in the future.

If you are in a school or college where there are other students following courses in leisure and tourism, you may wish to put on an exhibition of your event, to include:

i the planning of the event
ii the running of the event
iii the evaluation of the event
iv a brochure, prices, photographs, posters, a map showing the location etc.

A few members of the group can staff the stand and answer any questions asked about the event. If it was connected to the local community, you may also have publicity from the local newspaper or thank-you letters from people who benefited from the event.

An exhibition such as this is good publicity for your course, and you may be helping to put the minds of prospective students at ease, particularly if you enjoyed the event; or perhaps you will give them ideas for the future. You might be able to use some time in your communication lessons to help prepare your exhibition.

index

AA (Automobile Association) 28
ABTA (Association of British Travel Agents) 28
accident books 5
accommodation 11
ACE International (Association of Conferences and Events) 28
action plans 44–5, 73, 75
advertising 33
see also marketing; promotions
Alton Towers 9
American Adventure 9
applications for employment 22–3, 24–6
Arts Council 3
Association of British Travel Agents (ABTA) 28
Association of Conferences and Events (ACE International) 28
Association of Exhibition Organisers 28
Association of Teachers of Tourism 28
attitudes to customer care 51–2
attracting customers 9–10
Automobile Association (AA) 28

Bath 9
body language 53–4
body space 54
booking facilities 73
Britannia 60
British Association of Conference Towns 28
British Association of Tourism Officers 28
British Federation of Hotel, Guest House and Self Catering Association 28
British Hospitality Association 28
British Incoming Tour Operators Association 28
British Institute of Facilities Management 28
British Institute of Innkeeping 28
British Resorts Association 28
British Safety Council 29
British Spas Federation 29
British Standards Institute (BSI) 29
British Tourist Authority 29
British Tourist Board 3
brochures 38–40
Buckingham Palace 9
Business & Technology Education Council (BTEC) 29
business travel 11

Camping & Outdoor Leisure Association 29
car parks 4
cash rebates 41
cashiers, *see* receptionists
CBI (Confederation of British Industry) 29
charities 3
Chartered Institute of Marketing 29
Chessington World of Adventures 9
Chester Zoo 9
choosing activities 1, 4
City & Guilds of London Institute 29
closed questions 59
Colchester Zoo 42
committees 74, 75
communication skills 51, 53–5
complaint handling 59, 71, 76
Confederation of British Industry (CBI) 29
Confederation of Tourism, Hotel & Catering Management 29
costs
and profits 43
and sponsorship 45
of travel 11
Countryside Commission 3
curriculum vitae 19, 20–1
customer care
attitudes to 51–2
social skills 52–5

customer demand 10
customer needs 59
customer requirements 38, 41
customer service
  evaluating 59–68
  information provision 55, 56–7
  principles of 50
  and receptionists 17
  record keeping 68
  and sales techniques 58–9

deprived areas 3
desk research 36
directory of associations 28–9
disclaimer notices 4
discounts 41
disposable time 2
domestic tourism 5
Drayton Manor Park 9

economic benefits 1, 12
Edinburgh Castle 9
employment 12–29
  applications 22–3, 24–6
  areas of 12–14
  curriculum vitae 19, 20–1
  directory of associations 28–9
  interviews 22–3
  job directory 13–14
  job overlap 14
  qualifications 17–19
  receptionists 15–17
  reps 14, 58
  reservation clerks 14
  shift work 19
  statistics 13, 22
  with tour operators 14
  vacancies 22–3
European grants 3
evaluating
  customer service 59–68
  promotional campaigns 44
  team events 75–7
excursions 58
external communication 54–5
eye contact 54

face-to-face selling 58, 59
facial expression 54
facilities
  booking 73
  creating new 12
  quality of 6
  rationalising 32
feedback 36
field research 36
first-aid 4, 5
Flamingo Land 9
foreign-currency revenue 12
fund-raising 3

GNVQs (General National Vocational Qualifications) 18
government grants 3
Granada Studios 56–7
grants 3
growth in the industry 1

health questionnaires 27
heritage weekends 6
hospitality sector 15
hotel safe deposit facilities 4

incoming tourism 5
information 55, 56–7
internal communication 54–5
interviews 22–3

job descriptions 16–17
job directory 13–14
job overlap 14
job shadowing 19
Jorvik Viking Centre 9

Kew Gardens 9, 42, 57

learning 4
leisure breaks 5–6, 7
leisure time 1–2
lifeguards 4, 17
London Zoo 9
loss leaders 41

Madame Tussaud's 9

market research 36, 37, 44
market segments 38
marketing
  mix 34–6
  cycle 43
  function 33–4
meetings 73–5
minutes of meetings 74, 75
misrepresentation legislation 38

National Lottery 3
Natural History Museum 9
non-verbal communication 53–4, 55, 58
novelty value 9
NVQs (National Vocational Qualifications) 18–19

objectives of promotional campaigns 44
open questions 59
opening hours 43–4
opportunity trade 33
organising events 72–7

P&O 65–7
package tours 5
personal appearance 23, 58
personal belongings 4
place/location in marketing 34, 35
planning
events 72–7
promotions 43–5
playtime 2
posture 54
price
  of attractions 10
  in marketing 34, 35
  pricing strategy 41–3
  of travel 11
primary data 36
private sector 3
products 35–6, 36, 38
profits 3, 43
promotions 33, 36, 43–6
public sector 3
public-relations officers 36

qualifications 17–19
questionnaires
  on customer service 59–68
  foreign language 66–7
  market research 36

rationalisation 32
receptionists
  job description 16–17
  responsibilities 15–17
record keeping
  on customer service 68
  and event planning 75
recreation 1–2
reps 14, 58
reservation clerks 14
responsibilities of receptionists/cashiers 16–17
roles in life 52
Royal Academy 9

safe deposit facilities 4
safety 4–5
St Paul's Cathedral 9
sales promotions, *see* promotions
sales techniques 58–9
sandwich selling 58
Science Museum 9
secondary data 36
security
  of facilities 4–5
  of records 68
self-appraisal 16
service quality 11
services 35–6, 36, 38
shift work 19
social skills 52–5
special needs 10
special offers 41, 42, 58
sponsorship 3, 45
Sports Council 3
switchboard duties 17

target markets 44
teamwork 73–5
telephone sales 58–9
Thomson 61–4
Thorpe Park 9

timing in marketing 34, 35
tour operators 14
tourism, definition 5
Tower of London 9
Tower World 9
Trade Descriptions Act (1968) 38
trade magazines 23
training programmes 19
travel agents 8
travel costs 11
treasurers 74

verbal communication 53, 55
visitor attractions 9
voluntary organisations 3

weekend breaks 5–6, 7
Windsor Castle 9